FARBER BROTHERS KROME-KRAFT

A Guide For Collectors

By Julie Sferrazza

Additional copies can be ordered from:

ANTIQUE PUBLICATIONS
Division of Richardson Printing Corporation
P.O. Box 553
Marietta, Ohio 45750

*Dedicated to the memory of Louis and Harry Farber
and the many employees of Farber Brothers and The Sheffield Silver Company
who produced this beautiful ware, throughout the years.*

Krome·Kraft

PLATED HOLLOW WARE

FARBER BROTHERS
NEW YORK CITY

THE INSIGNIA OF FINEST
CRAFTSMANSHIP AND HIGH-
EST QUALITY IN CHROMIUM
PLATED HOLLOWWARE

CONTENTS

FORWARD

If you are a Farber Brothers collector, chances are you started your collection much the same way I did, with Cambridge glass set in Farber Brothers chrome holders. At first, I thought Cambridge to be the only supplier of inserts to Farber Brothers. As my collection grew, I discovered that many different china and glass manufacturers had furnished inserts to be used with Farber Brothers holders, rims and bases. Presented on the following pages is the result of over thirteen years of collecting and almost ten years of extensive research into the Farber Brothers story.

This book deals primarily with the products of Farber Brothers of New York, N.Y. manufactured after the introduction of their patented clip-on clip-off holder in 1932. It does not include the products of S.W. Farber (FARBERWARE®) of Brooklyn, N.Y. or Farber & Shlevin. Although blood relatives, there was never any corporate relationship between the three companies. The common mislabeling of Farber Brothes products as FARBERWARE®, trademark of the S.W. Farber Co., by collectors and dealers alike is an unintentional but confusing practice. It is my hope that this book will end some of the confusion.

This book is divided into three sections. Section I—Farber Bros. items with glass inserts. Section II—Farber Bros. items with china inserts. Section III—Farber Bros. items without glass or china inserts. I have tried to present as accurately as possible the name of each item, manufacturer of the insert, measurements of the item, colors in which the insert has been found, which metals were used in the manufacture of the holders and, in most cases, approximate years produced. Items not located in company catalogs have been given names to facilitate identification. These names are shown in quotation marks to distinguish them from names which were found in Farber Bros. catalogs. Whenever possible, item numbers were taken from original catalogs and placed in front of the item's name. These should aid in the advertising and selling of an item. You will notice that several of the pictures were taken directly from original catalogs. It was necessary to do this since it was impossible to locate every item needed to photograph.

After the description of each item, I have listed suggested values. These are not the final say for what you should pay for a piece or expect to sell an item for. They are based on what I have paid for items in my collection and what I have seen Farber Brothers products advertised for in trade papers and at glass shows in various parts of the country. Obviously, any damage to either the holder or the insert will reduce the price considerably.

In spite of my best efforts, this book cannot be 100% complete. There are many more pieces to be discovered and identified. I hope this book will be a valuable aid in your search for Farber Brothers items.

ACKNOWLEDGEMENTS

Researching a company that is no longer in existence can be extremely challenging. Most of the companies that supplied inserts throughout the 50 years of production at Farber Brothers have long since closed their doors. The few that are still operating, have given their time and information freely. Sadly, no records of any value survived the liquidation of Farber Bros. in 1965, with the exception of a few company catalogs. I would like to extend my gratitude and appreciation to the individuals and companies who have helped make my research easier. Many have answered questions, shared knowledge, brought previously unknown items to my attention and provided encouragement to make my dream of a book about Farber Brothers a reality.

Thank you, Diane Agosto, Helen Allen, Gene Allen, Brad Allen, Francis Bones, The Corning Glass Works, Bridgette Dezmain, Linda Dezmain, Dave Dura, Don Eisenberg, Kathleen Fex, The Fenton Art Glass Company, J.R. Haden, Fostoria Glass Company, Barbara Hellmann, Vic Hellmann, John M. House Town Historian, Pelham, N.Y., The Indiana Glass Company, Laverne Kiley, Gail Krause, Lenox Inc., Harriet Magee, Kathy Magee, Maxine Nelson, Louise Reem, Ferill Jeane Rice, Lianna Schon, Bill Schon, Ben Sferrazza, Dan Sferrazza, Paul Sferrazza, The Sheffield Silver Company, Elaine Storck, Blair and Cindy Stutz, Ray Taft, The Viking Glass Company, Clarence Vogel, The Westmoreland Glass Company, Loren Yeakley and the many china, glass and antique dealers across the country that have enhanced my collection.

Special thanks to: I.H. Farber, V.P. Sales and Office Management,
Farber Brothers/The Sheffield Silver Co. 1946-1973.

Sam Farber, V.P. Production,
Farber Brothers/The Sheffield Silver Co. 1949-1960.
for answering question after question and providing original catalogs that are used throughout this book.

Farber Brothers History

Farber Brothers, as the name suggests, was founded by two brothers—Louis and Harry Farber. Louis and Harry were born in Russia in the late 1800's and educated in Europe prior to immigrating to the United States. Neither man attended college, choosing instead to invest the years learning the trade that was to be the foundation of their future enterprise.

Prior to starting Farber Brothers, they gained invaluable experience in the metalcraft business as employees of their brother's firm, S.W. Farber Company. S.W. Farber, of Brooklyn, N.Y., was engaged in the manufacture of nickelplated and silverplated hollow-ware, along with aluminum, brass, and copper goods. These products were merchandised under the trade name, FARBERWARE®. When employed at S.W. Farber, Louis held a position in marketing and sales, while Harry directed production operations. The company that was their training ground went on to become a household name in the cookware and kitchen appliance industry. As for Louis and Harry, their future lay elsewhere.

In 1915, with their experience at S.W. Farber behind them, Louis and Harry established Farber Brothers. They founded their new company on an ideal to manufacture superior quality hollow-ware and brass goods to be sold at competitive prices—an ideal that was adhered to and which kept Farber Brothers successful for the next 50 years. They built an organization on customer service, customer satisfaction, and value. They were confident that there was no better product at the price.

The original Farber Brothers factory was located at 142 Grand Street, in lower Manhattan. The many New York City companies, devoted to metalcraft, provided healthy competition for their newly formed company and a pool of skilled craftsmen. By 1920, after being in business only five years, Farber Brothers was making their presence felt by other companies in the metalcraft industry, including S.W. Farber. An advertisement in the 1920 issue of the New York City edition of The Yellow Pages stated "Buy FARBERWARE from the original—S.W. Farber"—a clear indication that the Farber Brothers name had gained the recognition of the buying public. In subsequent issues of The Yellow Pages, it was common to find a single Farber Brothers advertisement sandwiched between two S.W. Farber advertisements.

In 1920, needing additional space, they purchased and occupied a building located at 13-15-17 Crosby Street. A six story brick structure, two blocks from their original site, this building served as both office and factory. They remained at this location until the company was dissolved in 1965. In addition to the Crosby Street headquarters, they maintained a showroom at 339 5th Avenue, New York City for over 20 years.

Most present day collectors know Farber Brothers best for their designs that incorporated glass and china inserts. In examining a catalog from the late twenties, it is interesting to note that, at that time, only 20-25% of Farber Brothers' products actually included glass or china inserts. Emphasis, during their early years, was placed on silverplated and nickelplated hollow-ware and solid brass goods. There was a greater variety of items in the silverplated hollow-ware line than in the nickelplated line. In silverplate, they sold fruit bowls, casseroles, meat platters, and every imaginable serving accessory in between. The nickelplated line was limited to casseroles, pie plates, serving trays, lamps, bowls, and smoking articles. Solid brass goods were further limited to smoking articles, candlesticks, cuspidors, jardiniers and umbrella stands.

When Harry, the older brother, died in 1929, the metalcraft industry was in the midst of major changes. The development of chromium plating in the twenties, meant that silver, once considered the only acceptable metal on the dining table, now had a new rival. The Farber Brothers product line of silverplated and nickelplated hollow-ware was replaced by similar items manufactured with chromium plating. It was the invention of the patented clip-on clip-off holder in 1932, that assured that hollow-ware, of any kind, would never again dominate Farber Brothers' sales. The newly designed Farber Bros. items that held glass and china inserts were appealing and innovative. They were easy to care for and required no polishing to preserve the lustrous finish. An added feature of the items that incorporated glass or china inserts, was that replacements could be purchased if accidentally broken or chipped. This feature was always stressed in Farber Brothers advertisements. Farber Brothers' new line was considered the utmost in practical elegance. The sleek, modern, metal holders, which added sparkle as well as protected the inserts, were greeted with immediate approval in the marketplace and set the direction of Farber Bros. products for many years to come.

Sales were brisk during the mid to late thirties and into the early forties for chromium plated hollow-ware, especially for the designs that held inserts. These years were extremely prosperous. Chromium plated ware had been well received by the public. Farber Brothers had become an established leader in the industry. The trademark, Krome-Kraft, had become synonymous with the finest craftsmanship and highest quality in chromium plating. Their products could be purchased at all major jewelry, gift, and department stores.

In 1935, Farber Brothers purchased The Sheffield Silver Company of Jersey City, New Jersey and relocated all operations to 17 Crosby Street. The newly acquired firm specialized in the manufacture of fine silverplated hollow-ware and sterling items. While under the ownership of Louis Farber, Sheffield Silver was maintained as a separate company. They introduced several silverplate and sterling items with glass inserts that incorporated the patented clip-on clip-off design. Some examples of these can be seen in the chapter on The Cambridge Glass Company.

World War II was a difficult time for both Farber Brothers and Sheffield Silver and production was severly affected. It was impossible to obtain the chrome, brass, copper, silver and other essential raw materials needed to continue normal operations. During the 1942-1945 time period, Farber Brothers was called upon to perform defense subcontract work, primarily stamping. Sheffield Silver, although also involved with subcontract work, may have been able to continue production of a few sterling and glass combinations.

The end of the war saw Farber Brothers launch an ad campaign, focusing on well known womens' magazines, such as Better Homes and Gardens and American Home.

The concept of "non-tarnishing chrome" was stressed over and over again in advertisements from 1946 until 1951, but by then consumer tastes had dramatically changed. Chrome no longer had the popularity it once did. As Farber Brothers' sales started to decline, more emphasis was placed on The Sheffield Silver Co. The tide had turned. Chromium plated ware, although still produced, did not dominate the metal giftware market as in previous years, and was no longer profitable. Silver recaptured the market it had lost to chrome during the 20's and 30's. Eventually, Sheffield Silver became the more profitable of the two companies and assumed the role of the parent corporation.

Farber Brothers sales further declined during the late fifties and early sixties. Very few new designs were created, but in the late fifties, in an effort to combat declining sales, several articles then being produced in chrome were introduced in solid brass. They were not the good sellers Farber Brothers had hoped for. These solid brass items, some with glass inserts, some without, initially sold well, but after a short period of time, perhaps one year, they lost their popularity as their chrome companions had. Farber Brothers efforts to survive were further hampered by the limited number of glass companies, still in operation during the late fifties and early sixties, who could supply inserts.

In 1965, Farber Brothers' operations ceased and only the Sheffield Silver Company remained. Sheffield Silver continued to produce quality silverplated hollow-ware at their Crosby Street location until 1973. In December of that year, they were sold to The Reed & Barton Silver Company of Taunton, Massachusetts, where fine silverplated hollow-ware is still produced under the name Sheffield Silver. The purchase price, which exceeded $200,000, included all raw materials, work in progress, and manufacturing supplies. Reed & Barton acquired all machinery, molds, tools/dies, and designs as well as the trademark of The Sheffield Silver Company. The newly relocated Sheffield Silver Co. was able to hold on to existing customers, as well as expand their distribution throughout the United States and establish new accounts in Europe.

So ends the story of Farber Brothers, but for collectors, the story is just beginning . . .

FROM THE HOTEL DISTRICT CROSBY STREET IS QUICKLY ACCESSIBLE BY ALL SUBWAYS CANAL STREET STATION OR BY THE BROADWAY SURFACE LINE ALIGHT AT GRAND STREET. IN EITHER CASE YOU HAVE BUT A BLOCK TO WALK TO THE FARBER BUILDING. IF YOU PREFER, JUST TELEPHONE CANAL 3688 A ND OUR AUTOMOBILE WILL CALL FOR YOU.

FARBER BROTHERS CROSBY STREET FACTORY CIRCA 1920

Farber Brothers Patents

Copies of original patents, #87496 and #1924011, each of which were granted for designs created by J.J. Wilmont of Montclair, New Jersey and assigned over to Louis Farber have been included. These patents were granted for the invention, design and production of the clip-on clip-off holder. Patent #87496 was filed for on April 15, 1932 and granted August 2, 1932. Patent #1924011 was filed for on March 31, 1933 and granted August 22, 1933. There is reason to believe that a patent application was filed for the Duchess Filigree

Aug. 2, 1932.   J. J. WILLMOTT   Des. 87,496

HOLDER

Filed April 15, 1932

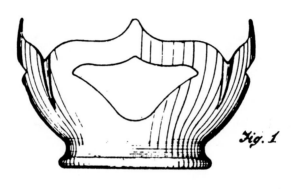

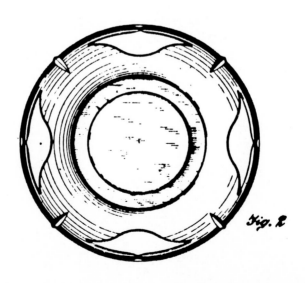

Fig. 1

Fig. 2

INVENTOR-

John Joseph Willmott

design but was never granted. Early Farber Bros. items which were based on that design can be found bearing a patent pending mark but later items bear either the original 1924011 patent number or Krome-Kraft trademark without patent numbers, depending on the type of item involved.

Small slips of paper bearing both patent numbers have been found placed between the insert and the holder of several Farber Brothers items. It appears this was done primarily on items bearing the Farber Brothers, New York, N.Y., Aug. 2nd, 1932 trademark. The holders on these items, were undoubtedly manufactured before the patent numbers were assigned. The addition of these slips of paper, may have been necessary to protect their patent rights.

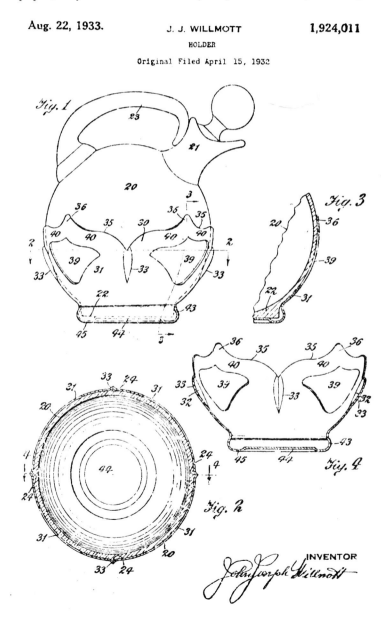

Aug. 22, 1933.   J. J. WILLMOTT   1,924,011
                                  HOLDER

                        Original Filed April 15, 1932

Major Holder Designs

From plain and simple to extremely detailed and intricate, Farber Brothers used a variety of designs on their holders and hollow-ware. Close ups of the most common can be found below. They are listed in order of importance and frequency of use.

No proper name was given to this cutout, the most common of all Farber Bros. designs. This design was the basis for the patented clip-on clip-off holder. Used from 1932 until 1965.

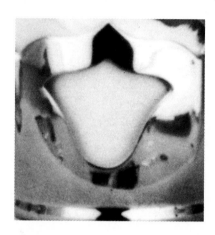

The proper name for this intricate design, as documented by old catalogs, is Duchess Filigree design. Traced back to as early as 1940, Farber Brothers items utilizing this design are pictured in catalogs until the early sixties. It appears that Farber Bros. tried to patent this design, since many items bear a patent pending mark. From all indications, the patent was never granted and Farber Brothers discontinued the use of the "patent pending" phrase.

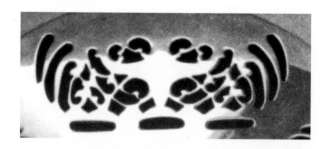

Used primarily on holders containing Westmoreland Lotus inserts, this cutout has been traced back to at least 1941. It was used for over twenty years.

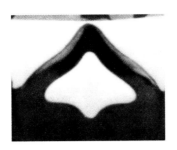

A complete line of chromium plated hollow-ware was offered by Farber Brothers based on this design. Referred to as the Lafayette design in original catalogs. Items based on the Lafayette design were well received and enjoyed a long period of production from approximately 1935-1965.

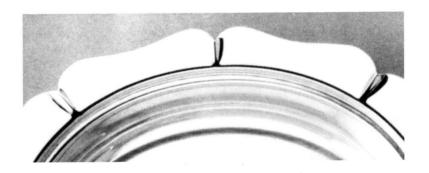

Rarely used on holders that contained an insert. Although you can find a 5½" compote in chrome or brass with a Cambridge glass insert utilizing this grape design. This cutout was used infrequently throughout the forties, fifties and into the early sixties. Referred to as Pierced Grape Design in original catalogs.

This particular cutout does not appear very often but is referred to as Perforated Lace Design by Farber Brothers. At the present time it has been found on just a few different holders containing Cambridge inserts. Also found on chrome and brass compotes and tidbits, without an insert, from the 40's, 50's and 60's.

Found solely on Farber Brothers chrome holders with Cambridge Glass inserts, this cutout design, due to a lack of catalog reference, does not have a proper name at this time. It was used rather infrequently by Farber Brothers and can be found on a total of only six different items during the thirties and possibly the forties.

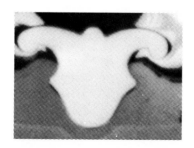

Identifying Trademarks, Paper Labels and Finial Shapes

A wide variety of trademarks were used during the fifty years of production at Farber Brothers. Fortunately for us, almost every item produced bears one of the identifying marks pictured on the following pages. Very few unmarked pieces will be found and should not be difficult to identify after consulting the chapter on major holder designs. Paper labels, identifying the manufacturer of the insert will occasionally be found on Farber Brothers items with Cambridge or Lenox China inserts.

It is rare to find inserts that bear a permanent identifying mark—in the mold or in the china glaze—that allows us to determine the manufacturer of the insert. Some items with Lenox, Fraunfelter China, Heisey and Vernon Kilns inserts, do have these marks. In these cases, the company trademark can be found on the underside or bottom of the insert. It is obvious from looking at original advertising and catalogs that Farber Brothers wanted the credit for designing and ultimately manufacturing the final product. In original company catalogs and advertisements, there are absolutely no references to the original supplier of the insert. In a few cases mention is made to the pattern name, but this is rare.

It appears that from the company's inception in 1915, Farber Bros. established a system of identification, using sequentially assigned numbers. How closely they adhered to this numbering system has yet to be determined. If they did, over 7000 different items were produced during the fifty years that Farber Brothers was in existence. Many early pieces can be found with the item number beneath the Farber Brothers mark.

Presented on the following pages are the many different trademarks you should encounter. Every effort was made to date the marks as accurately as possible. Emphasis was placed on the identifying marks used after the invention of the clip-on clip-off holder in 1932. Many of the marks listed contain the following symbols, (£), a familiar sight to most Farber Bros. collectors. The first symbol, (£), represents the British Pound Sterling, the second, , was used to denote quality craftsmanship and the third, , is a Fleur de Lis. It has been suggested by a relative of the founders, that these symbols may have been chosen because they looked like an L for Louis Farber and an H for Harry Farber. This set of marks was adopted early in the company's history, I believe prior to 1920. A small section on the paper labels and finial shapes that were used by Farber Bros. is also included. Armed with this information, you can now start identifying and dating your Farber Brothers collection.

Farber Brothers Trademarks

1) *This is the earliest known Farber Brothers mark. Used as early as 1915 and occasionally through 1930. Sometimes found with an item number beneath as shown. The No 101 signifies the original Farber Bros. catalog number for that item. This mark has been located on china plates with chrome rims, stamped on the back over the glaze, in gold or black ink.*

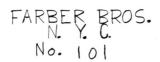

1)

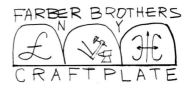

2)

2) *Used circa 1920 on silverplated hollow-ware, nickelplated ware and solid brass and copper goods. As a catalog from that time period states, "In adopting the name CRAFTPLATE we have put our signature, our personal guarantee, on every piece of hollow-ware made in the Farber Brothers factory—a three-fold assurance of Value, Service and Satisfaction. You can always recommend CRAFTPLATE with the confidence that there is none better at the price."*

3) *Registered trademark, U.S. Patent Office, No. 175,868 granted on November 13, 1923 for silverplated hollow-ware. In their application, Farber Bros. claimed use of the mark since January 26, 1923. Silver and nickel plated hollow-ware, copper, brass and mosaic gold items bear this mark that was in use from approximately 1923 until 1932. Beginning in the twenties, and continuing until approximately 1931, an entire line of clocks using the Silvercraft trademark was produced. Alarm clocks, easel clocks, pedestal clocks and even banjo clocks with 22 kt. rose or green gold plate or silverplate with an english or bright patina finish could be purchased.*

3)

4)

4) *Registered trademark, U.S. Patent Office, No. 317,913 granted on August 10, 1931, for silver and silverplated ware for domestic table use. First used by Farber Brothers in December of 1930. Chromium plated hollow-ware has also been found stamped with this mark from 1931-1933. Not extensively used.*

5) *There is a limited amount of information on this trademark and why it was chosen to be used. It obviously dates back to 1932, when the design patent, #87496 was already assigned, but before the mechanical patent #1924011, which relates to the invention and production of the holder was granted. In 13 years of collecting well over 1000 items, this mark has surfaced on only sugar and creamers, set in chrome holders, with Cambridge 3400/98 inserts.*

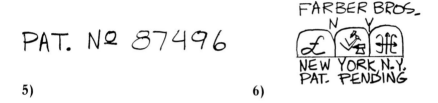

5)   6)

6) *Stamped on mosaic gold holders from the 1931-1932 time period while Farber Bros. was awaiting the patents for the clip-on clip-off holder to be approved. Also stamped on Duchess Filigree design items and holders, while awaiting a decision on the design patent application for the Duchess Filigree design.*

7) *Used for a short period of time, approximately one year, from mid 1932 until mid 1933. Stamped primarily on holders with Ebony Cambridge inserts. If you encounter Farber Brothers items with this trademark, you can be certain that you have one of the earliest articles designed and produced using the clip-on clip-off holder.*

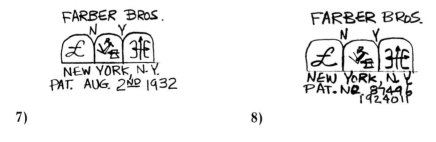

7)   8)

8) *The majority of all items produced will bear this familiar trademark. Used throughout the years of 1933-1965 on all types of items and all types of metals. In the case of chrome items, it appears that this mark was used from approximately 1933, until the late thirties when the Krome-Kraft name was adopted. Many solid brass holders from the late fifties and early sixties used this trademark.*

9) *Used during the same time period as trademark #8. Compotes, cocktails, sherbets, cordials and various other types of clip-on clip-off stemware will bear this mark. Located on the underside of the item, where the stem meets the foot. Often difficult to distinguish due to construction of the item or soldering in the area.*

9)

10)

10) *Not extensively used by Farber Brothers. Items that did not make use of the #87496 design patent for the standard clip-on clip-off holder, such as Duchess Filigree design decanters, can be found stamped with this mark.*

11) *The logo Krome-Kraft, was registered as a trademark on October 28, 1930, for chromium plated cooking, table and serving ware. It was used in advertising during the early 30's, but the phrase was not incorporated into the trademarks stamped on Farber Bros. articles until sometime in the late 30's. It is difficult to pinpoint the first year the trademark, Krome-Kraft was stamped on Farber Bros. items, but it can be accurately traced back to 1941 through available company catalogs. It is safe to assume that it was used a few years before that date. The trademark Krome-Kraft was renewed several times during the life of the company. It is interesting to note, a catalog from the early sixties does not make reference to Krome-Kraft at all.*

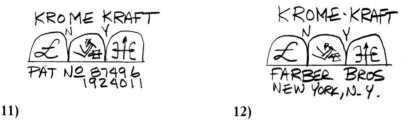

11)

12)

12) *Articles that did not make use of the patented clip-on clip-off holder, such as items with Farber Brothers rims, bases, trays and chromium plated hollow-ware will bear this mark.*

13) *Used during the same time period as trademark #12. Found primarily on designs with screw on Farber Brothers bases, such as Duncan & Miller items and also on several items, i.e. compotes and centerpiece/lazy susan, in which the base is easily removed to be used as a candlestick.*

13)

14)

14) Circa 1935-1950. Used on articles manufactured and marketed by The Sheffield Silver Company from sterling silver. Sheffield Silver items stamped with this mark made use of Farber Brothers patented clip-on clip-off holder design, hence the need for Sheffield Silver's trademark and both Farber Bros. patent numbers.

Paper Labels

The paper labels pictured below have been found on Farber Brothers solid brass holders, circa 1955-1965.

White background—Green lettering.

White background—Dark Green lettering and stripes.

Dark Green background—White lettering

White background—"SOLID BRASS" in Black. "MADE IN USA" and ♀ in Red.

This label was placed on articles and holders produced in mosaic gold.

Black background—Silver lettering

The paper label below was found on a 5912 silverplated high compote with Westmoreland Lotus insert. Although it is stamped with a Farber Brothers trademark, this paper label would tend to suggest that the 5912 high compote in silverplate may have been marketed by Sheffield Silver before, and possibly after, Farber Bros. was dissolved in 1965.

White background—Black lettering

Labels Found on Original Packaging

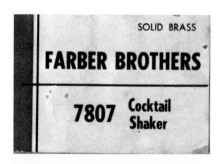

White background—Black lettering with a Dark Green stripe on the left side

Red and White lettering on Red and White background

Farber Brothers Finial Shapes

The following finial shapes have been included to aid in the identification of the occasional unmarked item that you may encounter and Farber Brothers lids and covers, since all are unmarked.

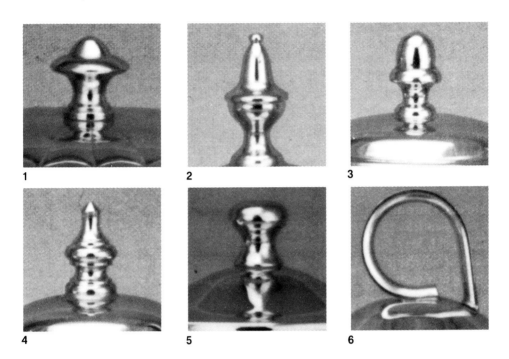

1   2   3

4   5   6

How Farber Brothers Holders Were Produced

Farber Brothers holders, lids and trays were manufactured through a series of stamping and finishing operations that started with blank stamping. Blank stamping produced the correct circle size of the base metal, primarily brass and sometimes copper. Next deep draw stamping was done. A series of up to four operations was necessary to achieve the desired depth and shape for some holders. After the basic form was completed, pierce stamping was performed to obtain the desired cutout design and trim the edges of the item. Trademarks and tray engravings were the result of yet another stamping operation. Cast or machined stems, finials, and handles were press fit and then soldered or wedged onto the main form to complete the designs.

Polishing was the next step. Polishing to remove imperfections in the metal and attain a smooth finish, was usually done with semi-automatic machines but sometimes accomplished by hand. The resulting article was then cleaned and prepared to be plated. Depending on the type of holder, a plating of chrome, nickel, silver, or 22 kt. gold was applied. Solid brass and copper objects did not require this final plating step, but instead were polished and lacquered to retain their brilliance.

Materials Used in the Manufacture of Farber Brothers Products

Mosaic Gold—

Farber Brothers name for holders that are gold in color and stamped out of metal that has a textured surface. Sometimes confused with solid brass holders, these holders are actually 22kt gold plated on solid brass. Introduced sometime during the early to mid thirties and discontinued prior to 1940. These were a good seller when introduced, after only a year or so their popularity faded. Used prior to 1932 on items that did not make use of the patented clip-on clip-off holder, such as trays, clocks and metal giftware items.

Mosaic Chrome—

Essentially the same as mosaic gold but with a plating of chrome instead of 22kt gold. Very scarce. I have encountered only one sugar and creamer in 13 years of collecting. Perhaps items made from mosaic chrome were experimental, unpopular with the buying public or marketed for only a brief period of time.

Nickelplate—

Used from approximately 1915 to 1932 in the manufacture of metal giftware items. A few nickelplated articles can be found containing glass and china inserts. They are casseroles, vegetable dishes, pie plates and beefsteak dishes.

Copper—

Farber Brothers ice buckets, silent butlers and chafing dishes without glass or china inserts can be found made from copper. Also used as the base metal to a few chromium plated hollow-ware items. Copper items were offered prior to 1930 and again during the early sixties. A pair of compotes with solid copper bowls and solid brass stems and bases is featured in the chapter on The Westmoreland Glass Company.

Pewter—

Items made from pewter date back prior to 1932. Pewter was not used extensively by Farber Bros. and only in the manufacture of items without glass or china inserts. Not used in the production of clip-on clip-off holders. Compotes, vases, candelabras, candlesticks, bon bon dishes, water pitchers, and fruit bowls made from pewter are waiting to be found.

Sterling—

Compotes, salt and peppers, cigarette urns and other items with sterling holders, rims and bases were produced after the acquisition of The Sheffield Silver Company in 1935. All the sterling items shown in this book were produced and marketed by Sheffield Silver. These items will bear the Sheffield Silver trademark and also the Farber Bros. patent numbers #87496 and #1924011. Although these sterling articles are not technically products of Farber Brothers, I am including them since they make use of the patented clip-on clip-off holder.

Chrome—

The common name for items that are actually chromium plated. The base metal is usually brass and sometimes copper. Used extensively from 1932 until 1965 in the production of clip-on clip-off holders and chromium plated hollowware. More Farber Bros. items will be found in chrome than in any other metal. Chrome was extremely popular because it never tarnished and did not need to be polished as with silverplate.

Brass—

Although chrome holders are more plentiful, Farber Bros. did produce several solid brass clip-on clip-off holders. Many of these were outfitted with a label that stated the holder was indeed solid brass, lacquered and should be cleaned with a soft cloth. Produced during the fifties and early sixties. From all indications, they were not especially good sellers. This could be the main reason why they are more elusive than their chrome counterparts. Some solid brass goods were produced prior to 1932. These items did not make use of the patented clip-on clip-off holder or contain inserts of any kind. Smoking articles, including ash receivers, cuspidors and tobacco jars were produced besides jardiniers, candlesticks and umbrella stands.

Silverplate—

Used extensively from 1915 to 1932 in the production of fine silverplated hollow-ware items and less frequently after 1932 in the manufacture of silverplated clip-on clip-off holders. Silverplated holders with glass or china inserts, today prove to be difficult to find. When found the plating is usually in poor condition, due to use and the age of the item.

Care of Your Farber Brothers Holders

When you buy a Farber Brothers item with an insert of glass or china, the first thing to do is gently separate the insert from the holder. It may be difficult to remove the insert, because many people didn't and still do not know that the inserts snap out for easy cleaning and replacement. Soaking in warm water should loosen and remove any dirt that has accumulated over the years.

Inserts, whether they are glass or china, can be cleaned with soap and water. Holders have to be cleaned according to the type of metal finish. Use a quality liquid or paste chrome or silver polish for your chrome and silver items—follow the manufacturer's directions. Solid brass objects were sold with a lacquer coating, intended to prevent tarnishing. After years of use, the lacquer finish can lose its effectiveness and it is likely that your solid brass objects will benefit from polishing with a quality brass polish. Mosaic gold holders, which are 24kt. plated on brass, present an interesting challenge. I find cleaning with a paste, silver polish works best. Farber Brothers items without glass or china inserts should be cleaned the same way and with the same products as your metal holders.

Since most Farber Bros. holders were actually plated, holders will often be found with varying degrees of damage. Occasionally, holders from salt shakers will be badly pitted, and often, after years of use, some of the plated holders will be worn down to the base metal. There is no way to reverse this damage except by replating, which can be done, but is extremely cost prohibitive. Another problem encountered by Farber Brothers collectors, is that sometimes the clip-on clip-off holders will be found split or cracked, especially down the center of the V-shaped crimps which are located around the holder. There is no certain explanation for this occurrence. A plausible reason is that one of the processes of forming the holders, deep draw stamping, left stress lines in the metal. A tight fitting insert—combined with the expansion and contraction of a holder, due to temperature changes—can exert enough pressure to cause a holder to crack along the stress lines. Some cracks are very obvious, while others are thin and hard to detect. Check the holder when buying Farber Brothers pieces—not just the insert. Remember, damage to either will reduce the value of any item.

Farber Brothers Items with Glass Inserts

Introduction

I know you will be surprised, as I was, at the number of different companies that supplied glass inserts to Farber Brothers from 1915 until 1965, and with the variety of items that were designed using those inserts.

Listed alphabetically are thirteen well known glass companies and the inserts which they furnished to Farber Brothers for 50 years. The Cambridge Glass Co. starts off the list and has the distinction of being the number one supplier of glass inserts. Cambridge furnished close to 80% of all the glass inserts bought by Farber Brothers. Fenton, Fostoria, Heisey, Imperial, Indiana, New Martinsville, Morgantown, Corning, Viking, Thermos, Westmoreland and Duncan & Miller made up the remaining 20%. The items shown in this section were designed after the invention of the clip-on clip-off holder in 1932. As you will see, the diversity of these items is endless.

In your search, you will probably encounter items, not pictured here, which were made prior to 1932. Before 1932, holders made of silverplate and nickelplate held various types of glass inserts, primarily clear in color. The inserts were not snapped into the holder as with most Farber Brothers items made later, but were set loosely into the holders or set on top of metal trays. Among the items produced prior to 1932 were casseroles, pie plates, vegetable dishes, sherbets, frappé and grapefruit sets. Several different style relishes and cheese and cracker dishes were also produced.

At the end of this section are Farber Brothers items having glass inserts of unknown origin. Eventually, many will be identified and added to the list of companies that are known to have furnished glass inserts, but I'm sure a few will lead us to discover other companies, such as Jeannette and Paden City, who may also have supplied inserts to Farber Brothers.

Cambridge

For almost 40 years, The Cambridge Glass Company of Cambridge, Ohio had the distinction of being the primary supplier of glass inserts to Farber Brothers. From approximately 1915, until the final closing of Cambridge in 1958, inserts from at least eight major Cambridge lines, in fourteen different colors and five different etchings, were sold to Farber Brothers.

Inserts of Amber, Amethyst, Forest Green, Royal Blue, Crystal, Carmen, Ebony, Milk, Pistachio, Dianthus Pink, Moonlight Blue, Heatherbloom, Mocha and Late Dark Emerald were used with Farber Brothers metal holders, rims, and bases. Catalogs and advertisements refer to the colors by more generic names such as clear, green, red, and blue. In addition to individual colors, cocktails, cordials, tumblers, and sherbets were offered in a "rainbow of six colors". The "rainbow" colors were Crystal, Amber, Amethyst, Forest Green, Royal Blue, and Carmen. Be aware that, due to replacement or switching of inserts, items shown may be found in colors and etchings other than those listed.

Many articles, with "green" inserts, were sold for periods of time which began prior to, and continued after, the introduction of Cambridge's Late Dark Emerald in 1949[1]. This makes it difficult to determine whether "green" inserts sold after that year are Forest Green or Late Dark Emerald. Although Forest Green was discontinued prior to the introdution of Late Dark Emerald,[1] there is little difference between "green" Farber Brothers products before and after 1949. In the listing section, "green" items known to be available after 1949 are referred to as Late Dark Emerald, although there is the possibility that Farber Brothers continued to buy Forest Green as a custom color. Items produced for extended periods both before and after 1949 are referred to as both, Late Dark Emerald and Forest Green.

Of all the colors, Amber and Amethyst are the most frequently found. Many items, with inserts of Amber and Amethyst, enjoyed prolonged periods of production and were sold long after other colors faded in popularity or were discontinued. In the range of prices given in the listing section, Amber and Amethyst are at the low end. Candleholders are a peculiar case for which Amber and Amethyst inserts are the most difficult to find.

The use of Pistachio, Dianthus Pink, Moonlight Blue, and Heatherbloom was confined to only a few different articles. It is impossible to base a collection on any of these colors. They are more of an oddity than a rarity, but a welcome addition to most every collection. Refer to the listing section to identify pieces available in these colors.

Inserts of Ebony, Milk, Carmen, and etched Crystal are generally difficult to find. Farber Brothers designs with inserts of Ebony and Milk were each manufactured for a limited span of time. Production of Ebony items was confined to the period from 1932 until 1940, while items with Milk inserts were offered only during the mid to late fifties. The colors were not popular when

---

[1]National Cambridge Collectors, Inc., Colors in Cambridge Glass, pg. 92, 1984.

introduced, which led to limited production and a small variety of items, hence the elusiveness of Ebony and Milk today. Inserts in Carmen or any of the etched patterns were more costly for Farber Brothers to purchase and that increase in cost was reflected at the wholesale and retail level as well. I can only presume that the higher prices of these items resulted in reduced sales versus the more plentiful colors. As one of the six "rainbow" colors, Carmen is no more difficult to find than other colors in flared and unflared cocktails and #5633, 12 oz. tumblers. Candleholders are also frequently found with Carmen inserts.

Of the five etchings located so far—Chantilly, Diane, Elaine, Rosepoint and Wildflower—Chantilly was, by far, the favorite. More Farber Brothers items have been found in Chantilly inserts than the other four etchings combined. For many years during the fifties, The Sheffield Silver Company made extensive use of articles with the Chantilly etching to which they added their sterling bases and accents.

Eight major Cambridge product lines are also represented. The 3126, 3400, 3500, Gyro-Optic, Pristine, Caprice, Tally-Ho and Nautilus lines were sold to Farber Brothers to be used as inserts in their designs. Bowls derived from the 3126 stemware line were widely used to fashion cocktails, cordials, tumblers, and sherbets.

Articles using the 3400 line are plentiful. The 3400 line is especially popular with today's collectors, due to its sleek, modern styling and excellent availability. It was more than a coincidence that the V-shaped crimps located on the outside of the Farber Brothers patented clip-on clip-off holders, were placed exactly to line up with the "rays" on the sides of most 3400 line items. The clip-on clip-off holder was clearly designed with the use of 3400 line inserts in mind. J.J. Wilmott's original mechanical patent pictures the 3400/92 ball decanter to illustrate the holder and how it functions. Specific reference is made to the locking action of the four rays on the decanter with the four crimps on the metal holder.

The use of the 3500 line by Farber Bros. was confined to the design of relish/preserve and buffet pieces. Prices on the 3500 items are minimal and all are easily found with the exception of the etched patterns.

The finding of Gyro-Optic, Pristine, Tally-Ho, and Nautilus inserts involves a little diligence, since they were not used extensively. Gyro-Optic was utilized during the early and mid 30's for just seven different items. Only ice tubs and relishes can be found in Pristine. The sole Tally-Ho article is a chrome handled, ice pail. Open salts are the only known objects designed using the Nautilus pattern.

Farber Brothers items designed using Caprice inserts have proven extremely difficult to find. Their scarcity and their beauty combine to make these items highly sought after and, by far, the most expensive of all the Farber Brothers/Cambridge combinations. Included in these items are, the #187 35 oz. Caprice decanter and #178 90 oz. Caprice Doulton Jug, both in Farber Brothers chrome Duchess Filigree design holders. If you are fortunate, you may locate one of the

Caprice vases, which were offered in various sizes with the standard, chrome clip-on clip-off holder. All of the above items can be found in Mocha, Amethyst, Royal Blue, Forest Green and perhaps Carmen, as well.

It is interesting to note, that the figure from the Cambridge 3011 Statuesque Line, commonly called "Nude Stem" by collectors, was used by Farber Brothers a short time after it was introduced by The Cambridge Glass Company in 1931. The #5566 "nude stem" compote was the first Farber Bros. design that incorporated this figure. The compote was introduced during the 1932-1933 time period, and was dropped from production between 1948 and 1953. Other items using the "nude stem" are as follows: 9″ chrome candlesticks with removable glass inserts; all-chrome compotes in 6″ and 7¼″ sizes; and 8″ all-chrome candlesticks.

It is apparent that Farber Brothers was one of the largest buyers of custom work from The Cambridge Glass Co. Approximately 75% of all inserts ordered were designed especially for use in Farber Brothers holders. Probably the most frequently supplied custom insert was the 5″ round compote insert. Farber Bros. took an otherwise plain and simple piece of glass and, with the use of their holders, transformed it into over 15 different designs, some of which were produced for more than 25 years of their 40 year relationship. The #5562 high compote is one such item. It was produced, using Cambridge inserts, from 1932 until the demise of The Cambridge Glass Co. in 1958. Production continued using Morgantown inserts, until 1965. Sales exceeded 400,000 units during Farber Brothers' history.

Very few of the Cambridge inserts which were furnished to Farber Brothers bear the Cambridge Glass Company △ trademark. In fact, to my knowledge, supported by a collection of over 1000 Farber Bros. items with Cambridge inserts, only the 7¼″ bowl in ebony with chrome base is marked with the familiar △ . Although this is true, almost all inserts furnished to Farber Brothers were shipped with Cambridge paper labels, and many items, even today, can be found with labels intact.

You may notice color variations between items with inserts of the same color. This is due in part to the thickness of the glass involved. Thicker items will appear darker, while thinner inserts will appear lighter. This is especially true with the transparent colors. A good example fo this is the color Amber. In addition to differences caused by variations in thickness, Cambridge Amber inserts supplied during the 1955-1958 time period will appear darker than the same inserts supplied in earlier years.

You may notice a discrepancy in the capacities of various decanters, glasses, and pitchers stated in the Cambridge listing of this book versus capacities found in published Cambridge literature. Volumes shown in this book are from Farber Brothers catalogs or actual measurements and I believe the discrepancies are due to the differences in the way the measurements are made, and not due to Farber Brothers specifying a special size.

The relationship between Farber Brothers and The Cambridge Glass Company, which endured for four decades, was crucial to the success of both. While the two companies have long since faded into the past, the unique designs which brought them together will live on.

Morgantown Glass Works

The final closing of the Cambridge Glass Company in 1958, presented the management of Farber Brothers with a huge dilemma: Who would replace Cambridge, their major supplier of glass inserts for the past forty years? Although the demand for Farber Brothers products was continually dropping and total sales were declining, many items with Cambridge inserts were still good sellers. These included compotes and cocktail sets, along with salt & peppers, sugars & creamers, and oil & vinegars from the 3400 line. Farber Brothers was faced with three options: 1) Discontinue the items that were currently being offered using Cambridge inserts when their supply of Cambridge inserts was exhausted; 2) Find another glass company to design new molds to produce replacements for the Cambridge inserts needed; 3) Get approval for another glass company to produce inserts using the original Cambridge molds. The end result was very close to their third option.

After a recommendation from Cambridge management, Farber Brothers approached the Morgantown Glass Works of Morgantown, West Va. to produce glass inserts for them. These inserts were manufactured using the same molds Cambridge had used to supply various inserts to Farber Bros. Cambridge transferred the molds to Morgantown and also provided glass batch formulas to match the colors produced by Cambridge. Morgantown did not put identifying marks, paper labels, or wrapping on the inserts they supplied to Farber Brothers. In fact, Morgantown was able to match the Cambridge colors so well that there is virtually no difference. Amber, Amethyst, Milk and Emerald inserts were produced, from the late fifties into the early sixties. Note that the color Emerald, as used to describe inserts supplied by Morgantown, is equivalent to the color commonly referred to by Cambridge collectors as Late Dark Emerald. See the Cambridge introduction for more information on Farber Brothers' "green" inserts. Mr. J.R. Haden, former production manager for Morgantown and Fostoria, supplied me with the above information and was also able to identify some of the shapes in which inserts were produced.

While this presents the "pure" Cambridge collector with a dilemma, the problem is minimized by the limited number of types and colors actually produced by Morgantown. Condiment, oil and vinegar, salt and pepper, and sugar and creamer sets with crystal, applied, handles are Cambridge in origin. The same sets, with colored, applied, handles, may be either Cambridge or Morgantown in origin.

Those items in the listing with the "Cambridge/Morgantown" notation are known to have been originally produced by Cambridge and eventually by Morgantown. In a few instances where it is uncertain whether Morgantown reproduced the insert, credit is given only to The Cambridge Glass Company.

Morgantown also provided a few inserts clear in color to Farber Brothers during the same time period. These were not made using Cambridge molds but were original designs worked out between Farber Brothers and Morgantown. They are reportedly a footed salt and pepper, oil and vinegar and possibly a cheese shaker. I have not been able to locate these items, so be on the lookout for them.

Cambridge Listing

Butterdishes/Bon-Bons/Candy Dishes

5567 Double Bon-Bon—Page 97-1, 2, 4
Cambridge Glass Co. Height 6". Length 12". Offered in the following colors: Amber, Amethyst, Forest Green, Royal Blue and Carmen. Holders found in chrome and mosaic gold. Approximate years of production, 1933-1940. Discontinued prior to 1941. Difficult to find in mosaic gold. *Suggested Value: Chrome $35-45. Mosaic Gold $45-55. With Carmen inserts, add 50% to the above prices.*

5560 Bon-Bon—Page 97—3, 5
Cambridge Glass Co. Diameter 5½". Height 2¼". Inserts of Amber, Amethyst, Forest Green, Royal Blue and Carmen in chrome or silverplated holders. Offered from 1933 into the early 40's. Carmen is the most difficult color to find. *Suggested Value: Chrome $20-25. Silverplate $25-30. Carmen inserts command a higher price, 50% more.*

5777 Butterdish—Page 97-6
Cambridge Glass Co. 3500/129. Dimensions: 5½" x 5½". Height overall: 2¼". Inserts of Amber, Amethyst, Forest Green, Royal Blue, Crystal and Elaine etched. Farber Bros. holder found in chrome with raised tulip design in each corner. Came complete with butter spreader. Offered during the early forties. *Suggested Value: $12-18. Elaine etched $25-30.*

"Butterdish"—Page 97-7
Cambridge Glass Co. Dimensions: 8¾" x 5" x 1¼". Insert 4" x 4". Chrome Duchess Filigree design handled tray comes with a slot in the rear to rest a butter knife. Only Moonlight Blue and Amethyst inserts have surfaced. Look for other colors to be found. May have originally been sold with a chrome lid. *Suggested Value: $18-22.*

The **5564 candy/butterdish,** while retaining the same catalog number, was restyled several times from the 30's through the 50's. Following is a listing of three styles:

33

5564 Candy/Butterdish — Not pictured, Same finial as Page 23-2

Cambridge Glass Co. Diameter 5½". Inserts of Amber, Amethyst, Forest Green, Royal Blue and Carmen. Offered by Farber Brothers for approximately ten years beginning in 1932, in chrome only. *Suggested Value: $25-30. With Carmen inserts, 50% more.*

5564 Butterdish — Page 97-8, 10

Cambridge Glass Co. Diameter 5½". Height 4½". Amber, Amethyst, Forest Green, Royal Blue and Carmen inserts in chrome Farber Brothers holder with domed lid and loop handle. Introduced in the late thirties. Not especially difficult to find. *Suggesed Value: $25-30. Carmen 50% more.*

5564 Chrome — Candy/Butterdish — Page 97-9
7564 Brass

Cambridge Glass Co./Morgantown Glass Works. Diameter 5½". Height 3½". This versatile candy/butterdish with "umbrella" design on lid was offered in chrome from approximately 1948 until 1965 with inserts of Amber, Late Dark Emerald and Amethyst. The brass version was offered during the late fifties and into the mid 60's, with inserts of Amber, Milk, Amethyst, Emerald. Morgantown provided Amber, Milk, Amethyst, and Emerald inserts from the late 50's until the mid sixties. More difficult to locate in brass than in chrome. *Suggested Value: Chrome $25-30. Brass $35-45.*

5780 Butterdish — Page 97-11, 12

Cambridge Glass Co. 3500/131. Dimensions: 6¾" x 4¾". Height overall 2¼". Choice of Amber, Amethyst, Forest Green, Royal Blue, Crystal and Chantilly etched inserts in chrome Farber Bros. holders. Produced during the forties. Not difficult to find with the exception of etched inserts. *Suggested Value: $15-18. Chantilly etched $25-30.*

"Butterdish" — Page 97-13

Cambridge Glass Co. Dimensions overall: 5¾" x 8¼" x 3". Insert 4½" x 6½". Crystal butterdish with "floral design" cut into the cover is the only color insert found to date. Farber Brothers chrome tray features a cutout design with engraved flowers. Offered during the late 40's, perhaps into the 50's. Although the insert to this butterdish bears a Cambridge paper label, I have sincere doubts that it was produced by them. It may be a product of the Viking Glass Co. *Suggested Value: $30-35.*

5742 Butterdish — Page 97-14

Cambridge Glass Co. 3500 line. Diameter 6¾". Pictured in a 1941 catalog in Crystal only, although other colors may be found, such as Amber, Amethyst, Forest Green and Royal Blue. Chrome base and cover with either a red or white plastic knob. Produced during the early forties. *Suggested Value: $18-22 in Crystal/Amber/Amethyst. Royal Blue $25-30.*

Candlesticks

"Candelabra" — Page 98-1, 2, 4
Cambridge Glass Co. Height 8½". Width 9½". Royal Blue, Amethyst, Crystal, Carmen and Amber inserts have surfaced. These candelabras are difficult to find with inserts of Amber and Amethyst. Originally sold in pairs during the late 30's with chrome holders only. *Suggested Value: $55-65/pair.*

5670 Two Lite Candelabra — Page 98-3, 5
Cambridge Glass Co. Base diameter 7¼". Height 5". Crystal, Royal Blue, Carmen, Amber and Amethyst inserts can be found. Farber Brothers Duchess Filigree design holders found in chrome only. Not easy to find with inserts of any color. Could be purchased separately or as part of a console set during the early forties. *Suggested Value: $45-55/pair.*

5660/69 Console Set — Page 98-6
Cambridge Glass Co. This Duchess Filigree design console set consists of the 11½" diameter, 5660 centerpiece and screen plus a pair of 5669 candlesticks that have removable glass candleholders. Produced during the late thirties and into the early forties with inserts of Amber, Amethyst, Royal Blue, Crystal and Carmen. A similar console set, #5661/70 was produced by Farber Bros. in the same colors but with two-lite candlesticks. *Suggested Value: With one-lite candlesticks: $70-80. With two-lite candlesticks: $80-90.*

"Candlesticks" — Page 98-7, 9
Cambridge Glass Co. Height 6⅝". Diameter at base 4". Farber Brothers chrome holder with embossed tulip design on each base. Inserts of Crystal, Royal Blue, Carmen, Amethyst and Amber were possibly produced during the late forties. *Suggested Value: $30-40/pair.*

5669 Candlesticks — Page 98-8
Cambridge Glass Co. Height overall 3¾". Base diameter 6". Crystal, Royal Blue, Carmen, Amethyst, and Amber inserts in chrome Duchess Filigree design holders, were made during the 40's and perhaps earlier. Surprisingly, Amethyst and Amber inserts have been the hardest to find. Offered in Crystal and Carmen in a 1941 catalog. Not certain when other colors were offered. *Suggested Value: $35-45/pair.*

Cocktails, Wines, and Cordials

Most of the drinkware pictured was originally sold as part of cordial, tumbler, decanter or cocktail sets. I am cataloging them individually, since that is the way they are most commonly found today.

5461 Cocktail—Page 99-1, 3, 5, 7
Cambridge Glass Co./Morgantown Glass Works. Height 5⅞". Capacity 3 oz. Mosaic gold, chrome, brass, and silverplate holders can be found with inserts of Amber, Amethyst, Forest Green, Carmen, Milk, Crystal, and Crystal with a wheel cut flower design. Chrome holders were produced from 1932 to 1965 and today are easily found. Mosaic gold and silverplate had a limited period of production. Both were discontinued before 1941, and therefore are difficult to find. The brass holders were manufactured from the late fifties into the early sixties and were not very popular—making them also difficult to find. All versions of this cocktail could be purchased as a set of six in a display box. Morgantown produced Amethyst, Amber, Emerald and Milk inserts from the late fifties into the early sixties. *Suggested Value: Chrome $8-10. Silverplate $12-14. Brass or Mosaic Gold $18-20.*

6095 Cocktail—Page 99-2, 6
Cambridge Glass Co. Height 6½". Capacity 3 oz. Farber Bros. chrome holder with a petal design on the foot and underside of the bowl. Amber, Amethyst, Chantilly etched and Wildflower etched inserts can be found. Wildflower etched inserts, are only etched from the top rim to where the holder starts, while Chantilly cocktails are etched over the entire bowl. These cocktails were available from the early forties until the mid fifties. Wildflower etched inserts were discontinued before 1946 and today prove to be the most difficult to find, followed by the Chantilly etched. *Suggested Value: Amber and Amethyst $12-$14. Etched $20-22.*

"Cocktail"—Page 99-4
Cambridge Glass Co. Height 7⅞". Capacity 5½ oz. Inserts of Amber, Amethyst, Forest Green, Royal Blue, Crystal and Carmen can be found in chrome holders. This cocktail is not easily found. *Suggest Value: $20-25.*

"Wine"—Page 99-8
Cambridge Glass Co. Height 5⅞". Capacity 2 oz. Holders made of chrome were produced for a period of almost twenty years, beginning in 1932. Inserts of Amber, Amethyst, Forest Green, Royal Blue, Carmen, Crystal and Ebony can be found. Ebony and Carmen are the most difficult to locate. From all indications, this wine glass was only offered with Ebony inserts for a limited number of years, during the mid to late thirties. *Suggested Value: $10-12. Carmen/Ebony $20-25.*

5460 Cordial—Page 99-9

Cambridge Glass Co. Height 4¼″. Capacity 1 oz. Farber Bros. holders of chrome and brass can be found with flared inserts of Amber, Amethyst, Forest Green, Royal Blue, Late Dark Emerald, Carmen, Crystal, Ebony and Milk. Produced in chrome from 1940 through 1955. Could be purchased in sets of six, with chrome holders during the early forties. Available with brass or chrome holders during the late 50's. Difficult to find in Carmen, Ebony or Milk. *Suggested Value: Chrome $8-10. Brass $12-16. With inserts of Ebony or Milk $16-22.*

"Cocktail"—Page 99-10

Cambridge Glass Co. Height 5⅜″. Capacity 3 oz. Chrome holder with a choice of Amber, Amethyst, Forest Green, Royal Blue, Crystal, Carmen, Dianthus Pink or Late Dark Emerald inserts. Offered from the mid 30's through the 50's. *Suggested Value: $8-10.*

6018 Cocktail—Page 99-11

Cambridge Glass Co. Height 4¼″. Capacity 3 oz. In 1941 they were sold in boxed sets of six, in the following colors: Amber, Amethyst, Forest Green, Royal Blue, Crystal and Carmen. A rainbow set (one of each color) could also be purchased. Farber Brothers chrome holder has a hollow pedestal base with concentric rings. An easily found item that enjoyed almost twenty years of production. *Suggested Value: $8-10 each.*

"Wine"—Page 99-12

Cambridge Glass Co. Height 3½″. Capacity 3 oz. Amber, Amethyst, Chantilly etched and Wildflower etched inserts can be found in chrome holders. Similar to the 6095 cocktail, minus the stem, with the holder resting directly on the foot. As with the 6095 cocktail the foot has a petal design. Wildflower inserts are the most difficult to locate with Chantilly etched ones a close second. Approximate years of production: Wildflower, only the early forties; Amber, Amethyst and Chantilly etched, the 40's through the mid 50's. *Suggested Value: Amber and Amethyst $10-12. Etched inserts $18-20.*

"Wine"—Page 99-13

Cambridge Glass Co. Height 3½″. Capacity 4½ oz. Your choice of Amber, Amethyst, Forest Green or Royal Blue inserts in chrome holders. Offered during the forties. *Suggested Value: $10-12.*

"Wine"—Page 99-14

Cambridge Glass Co. Height 4⅛″. Capacity 4½ oz. Farber Bros. footed, chrome holders with inserts of Amber, Amethyst, Forest Green and Royal Blue can be found. Produced during the early forties. *Suggested Value: $10-12.*

"Wine"—Page 99-15

Cambridge Glass Co. 3400/92. Height 2½". Capacity 2 oz. A familiar item to most collectors, this wine was produced in both chrome and mosaic gold. Known colors: Amber, Amethyst, Forest Green, Royal Blue, Late Dark Emerald, Carmen, Crystal, Ebony and Mocha in Gyro-Optic pattern. Chrome was produced from 1932 until the late fifties. The mosaic gold holders were dropped from production before 1940, making them scarce. *Suggested Value: Chrome $6-8. Mosaic Gold or chrome with Ebony insert $12-14.*

"Cordial"—Page 99-16

Cambridge Glass Co. Height 2⅞". Capacity 1 oz. This cordial has been found only in chrome, with the following color inserts: Amber, Amethyst, Forest Green, Royal Blue, Carmen, Crystal and Ebony. Offered by Farber Brothers during the early forties. *Suggested Value: $8-10. With Ebony inserts $16-20.*

"Cordial"—Page 99-17

Cambridge Glass Co. Height 4". Capacity 1 oz. Chrome holders only, with inserts of Amber, Amethyst, Forest Green, Royal Blue, Carmen and Crystal. This unflared cordial has been harder to find than the #5460 flared version. *Suggested Value: $8-10. Carmen $16-18.*

"Cordial"—Page 99-18

Cambridge Glass Co. Height 3". Capacity 1 oz. Chrome holders only, with inserts of Amber, Amethyst, Forest Green, Royal Blue, Carmen and Crystal. Produced during the late thirties. *Suggested Value: $8-10. Carmen $16-18.*

"Cordial"—Page 99-19

Cambridge Glass Co. #1900. Height 2". Capacity 1 oz. Choice of Amber, Forest Green, Amethyst, Royal Blue, Crystal, Carmen, Moonlight Blue, or Crystal with a wheel cut "thatched" design on the top half of the insert, in chrome Farber Bros. holders. Produced from approximately 1940 through the 50's. *Suggested Value: $6-8. Carmen/Moonlight Blue $8-10.*

Tumblers/Sherbets

5633 Tumbler—Page 100-1, 3
Cambridge Glass Co. Height 5″. Capacity 12 oz. This tumbler was offered by Farber Bros. in chrome or brass holders with inserts of Amber, Amethyst, Forest Green, Royal Blue, Crystal, Carmen, and Milk. Chrome produced during the forties and fifties, while brass holders were offered during the fifties. In 1941, the chrome version of this tumbler was sold in sets of six in a display box, complete with six glass muddlers with which to stir your drinks. All of one color, or a rainbow of one Amber, one Amethyst, one Royal Blue, one Forest Green, one Carmen and one Crystal. Milk inserts can be difficult to find. All other colors are plentiful. *Suggested Value: Chrome $10-12. Brass or with Milk inserts $18-22.*

5614 Tumbler—Page 100-2, 4
Cambridge Glass Co. Height 3½″. Capacity 6 oz. Inserts of Amber, Amethyst, Forest Green, Royal Blue, Crystal, Carmen and Milk can be found in chrome and brass holders. Proves more difficult to find than the 12 oz. version. Referred to as "old fashioned glasses" in a 1941 catalog, these tumblers were offered in chrome during the 40's and 50's and brass during the 50's. A stemmed version of this tumbler was also produced in chrome during the same time period and in the same colors. *Suggested Value: Chrome $8-10. Brass or with Milk inserts $16-20. Stemmed version in chrome $12-15.*

Tumbler—Page 100-5
Cambridge Glass Co. 3400/112. Height 4¼″ Capacity 8 oz. Inserts in Amber, Amethyst, Forest Green, Royal Blue, Ebony, Carmen, and Mocha in the Gyro-optic pattern can be found encased in both chrome and silverplated Farber Brothers holders. First sold in 1932, this tumbler was discontinued sometime before 1940. *Suggested Value: Chrome $10-12. Silverplate $12-14. With Ebony/Carmen inserts $18-22.*

Tumbler—Page 100-6
Cambridge Glass Co. Height 3½″. Capacity 6 oz. One of the first tumblers designed after the invention of the clip-on clip-off holder in 1932. This tumbler is commonly mistaken for a mustard without the lid. Produced from approximately 1932 to 1940 in chrome, with a choice of Amber, Amethyst, Forest Green, Royal Blue, Carmen and Ebony inserts. *Suggest Value: $8-10. Ebony/Carmen $15-18.*

"Sherbet Set"—Page 101-1
Cambridge Glass Co. Height 2⅝″. Diameter 3½″. Six sherbets with inserts of Amber, Amethyst, Forest Green, Royal Blue, Carmen, Dianthus Pink, or Mocha in the Gyro-Optic pattern, can be found on a 16½″ x 9″ chrome tray. In 1933, this set had a suggested retail price of $13.50. due to a limited production, this sherbet set proves difficult to find. *Suggested Value: $45-50. Carmen 50% more.*

"Seafood or Fruit Cocktail"—Page 101-2

Cambridge Glass Co. Height 4¼″. A rare and unusual item that was originally sold in sets of four or six. Inserts of Amber, Amethyst, Forest Green, Royal Blue, Crystal, and possibly Carmen can be found encased in chrome holders. A Crystal 4 oz. cup tops off this cocktail. *Suggested Value: $30-35 each.*

"Beverage Set"—Page 101-3

Cambridge Glass Co. Ten piece beverage set, circa 1933, in chromium plated holders. Could be purchased with inserts of Amber, Amethyst, Forest Green, Royal Blue, Carmen and Ebony. Tray size: 12″ x 18″. Ice pail is the familiar Tally-Ho pattern. This set had a suggested retail price of $37.50 in 1933. Dropped from production before 1939. *Suggested Value: $135-145. Carmen/Ebony $185-200 if complete.*

5462 Sherbet—Page 101-4

Cambridge Glass Co. Height 3¾″. Capacity 6 oz. Sold in sets of six in the following colors: Amber, Amethyst, Forest Green, Royal Blue, Carmen and Crystal, or a rainbow set with one of each color. Also found in Chantilly etched. A good seller for Farber Brothers, these sherbets were offered with chrome holders. Produced during the early 40's and perhaps even earlier. Sets with non-etched inserts can be easily acquired today. Sherbets with Chantilly etching are the most difficult to locate. During 1934, a stemmed version of this sherbet was sold with chrome or silverplated holders and inserts of Amber, Amethyst, Forest Green, Royal Blue, Crystal or Carmen. *Suggested Value (stemmed or unstemmed): $12-14. Chantilly etched or Carmen inserts $18-22.*

"Bridge Set"—Page 102-1

Cambridge Glass Co. 3500 line. Farber Brothers chrome handled tray holds four Farber Brothers #5633, 12 oz. tumblers with chrome holders, along with a 2 part Cambridge 3500 line insert. Dimensions: tray is 8½″ x 12″, height to top of handle 6¾″; insert is 3¾″ x 7″ x 1¼″. Choice of Amber, Amethyst, Royal Blue, Late Dark Emerald and Crystal inserts. *Suggested Value: $65-75.*

"Tumbler Set—Page 102-2

Cambridge Glass Co. Farber Brothers, chrome, T-handled tray with engraved floor, holds eight Farber Bros. #5614, 6 oz. tumblers, with chrome holders. Complete with drink stirrers. Dimensions: tray is 6¾″ x 13″, height to top of handle 10¼″. Mix or match the following insert colors: Amber, Amethyst, Forest Green, Royal Blue, Crystal or Carmen. Probably produced during the early forties. *Suggested Value: $95-105.*

Cordial/Wine Sets

5723 Cordial Set—Page 103-1

Cambridge Glass Co. Tray dimensions: 5½″ x 8″; height 5″. Six chrome encased 1½ oz. cordials in either Amber, Amethyst, Forest Green, Royal Blue, Carmen, Crystal or a rainbow of six colors were placed on an oval, handled, chrome tray. Tray will be found with either a white plastic knob or metal ring handle and has indents stamped in it for each glass to sit. Offered by Farber Bros. during the forties. A similar item 5722 was also offered. Same as above except the cordials are supplied without the patented clip-on clip-off holders. *Suggested Value: $35-40. Carmen $55-60.*

"Cordial Set"—Page 103-2

Cambridge Glass Co. Decanter 3400/119. Height to top of handle 4½″. Capacity 12 oz. Cordial #1341. Capacity 1 oz. Inserts of Amber, Amethyst, Forest Green, Royal Blue, Carmen, and Ebony in chrome or mosaic gold Farber Bros. holders, surrounded by six cordials. Cordials could be purchased to match the color of the decanter or, very often, the buyers mixed and matched colors to their liking. For example, 2 Amber, 2 Carmen, and 2 Royal Blue cordials with an Amethyst decanter. Circa late 30's. *Suggested Value: Chrome $55-65. Mosaic Gold $65-75 Carmen/Ebony $115-125.*

"Wine Set"—Page 103-3

Cambridge Glass Co. Tray dimensions: 7¾″ x 5¾″. Consists of six 2 oz. wines with chrome holders, on a round, ring handled, chrome tray. Inserts of Amber, Amethyst, Forest Green, Royal Blue, Carmen and possibly Ebony can be found. *Suggested Value: $35-45. Carmen/Ebony $60-70.*

5409 Cordial Set—Page 103-4

Cambridge Glass Co. Decanter 3400/119: height to top of handle 4½″; capacity 12 oz. Cordials: height 2⅞″; capacity 1 oz. Tray: 12½″ x 7¾″. Decanter inserts of Amber, Amethyst, Forest Green, Royal Blue, Carmen and Ebony. Cordials could be purchased in the following colors—Amber, Amethyst, Forest Green, Royal Blue, Carmen, Crystal and Ebony, to match the color of the decanter or any color combination desired. Offered through the late thirties and the early forties. *Suggested Value: $75-80. Carmen/Ebony $155-165.*

5791 Cordial Set—Page 103-5

Cambridge Glass Co. Decanter: height 12″; capacity 14 oz. Cordials: height 5″; capacity 1 oz. Offered during the 40's into the 50's, with inserts of Amber, Amethyst, Forest Green, and Royal Blue. Choice of six cordial glasses to match the color of the decanter, or with crystal bowls and stems with only the footed base to match the color of the decanter. Chrome Duchess Filigree design holder on decanter. Entire set rested on a 14″ chrome Duchess Filigree design tray. Commonly found in Amber and Amethyst. *Suggested Value: Amber/Amethyst $80-90. Forest Green/Royal Blue $125-135.*

5792 Cordial Set—Not Pictured. Similar to 5791, only larger.

Cambridge Glass Co. Decanter: height 14"; capacity 30 oz. Cordials: height 5"; capacity 2 oz. Offered during the 40's into the 50's, with inserts of Amber, Amethyst, Forest Green, and Royal Blue. Choice of six cordial glasses to match the color of the decanter, or with crystal bowls and stems where only the footed base matches the color of the decanter. The set was placed on a 16" Duchess Filigree design chrome tray. The holder on the decanter is also the Duchess Filigree design. *Suggested Value: Amber/Amethyst $125-135. Forest Green/Royal Blue $145-165*

5408 Junior Cordial Set—Page 103-6

Cambridge Glass Co. Decanter 3400/119. Height to top of handle 4½". Capacity 12 oz. With 2" high #1900 cordials. Capacity 1 oz. Tray 10" x 8½". This junior cordial set was offered by Farber Brothers during the mid thirties and into the early forties. Can be found with inserts of Amber, Amethyst, Forest Green, and Royal Blue in chrome and silverplated holders. Inserts of Carmen and Ebony are possible. The cordials to this set, could be purchased with or without holders. *Suggested Value: Chrome $60-70. Silverplate $70-75.*

5410 Cordial Set—Page 103-7, 9

Cambridge Glass Co. Decanter 3400/156: height 8"; capacity 12 oz. Cordial: height 4¼"; capacity 1 oz. This cordial set dates back to the late thirties and was offered for sale until the late fifties. Produced in both chrome and brass holders with inserts of Amber, Amethyst, Forest Green, Royal Blue, Carmen, Ebony and Milk. The cordials were sold to match the color of the decanter, or as a rainbow of six colors—one each of Amber, Amethyst, Forest Green, Royal Blue, Crystal and Carmen, could be purchased. The chrome version of this cordial set was originally sold on a 15½" x 8½" oval tray, while the brass version was sold on a round Milk tray trimmed in brass. *Suggested Value: $70-75. Brass or with Carmen/Ebony $165-175.*

1 Cordial Set—Page 103-8

Cambridge Glass Co. Decanter 3400/156: height 8"; capacity 12 oz. Cordials: height 4¼"; capacity 1 oz. Amber and Amethyst inserts in chrome holders are the only colors offered in a 1953 catalog. I suspect other colors such as Late Dark Emerald, Royal Blue, and Carmen can be found. *Suggested Value: $55-60 in Amber/Amethyst.*

Cocktail Sets

5775 Cocktail Set—(early design)—Page 104-1

Cambridge Glass Co. 1½ qt. chrome cocktail shaker with orange or walnut colored catalin handle and trimmings. Cocktails: height 5⅜″; capacity 3 oz. Tray: 16½″ x 9½″. Circa early forties. Choice of Amber, Amethyst, Forest Green, Royal Blue, Crystal and Carmen inserts, six of one color or a rainbow set with one of each color. *Suggested Value: $75-85.*

6093 Cocktail Set—Page 104-2; 105-1, 2

Cambridge Glass Co. 1½ qt. chrome cocktail shaker with six 3 oz., cocktails in "pierced" design chrome holders. Choice of Amber, Amethyst or Chantilly etched cocktail inserts. Round chrome tray with wheat border design. Diameter 15½″. Offered during the late 40's into the late 50's. In 1950, the stemmed version of this cocktail set, with Amethyst inserts, sold for $36.00. By 1953, Chantilly etched inserts were no longer offered. A similar version of this cocktail set also was offered with 3½″ high cocktails. Both sets are pictured. *Suggested Value: $90-95 with either high or low version of cocktails. Chantilly etched 50% more.*

5468 Cocktail Set—Page 104-3

Cambridge Glass Co. Cocktail shaker: 3400 line; height 11″; capacity 3 pints. Cocktail glasses: height 5⅞″; capacity 3 oz. Tray: 19½″ x 12″. This cocktail set dates back to the mid thirties. Offered in Amber, Amethyst, Forest Green, Royal Blue, Ebony and possibly Carmen in chrome holders. Discontinued before 1940, this set proves difficult to find. *Suggested Value: $130-140. Carmen/Ebony $185-195.*

5990 Cocktail Set—(late design)—Page 105-3

Cambridge Glass Co./Morgantown Glass Works. 1½ qt. chrome cocktail shaker with black composition handle. Six 3 oz. cocktail glasses with patented chrome holders. Chrome tray: 15½″ diameter. Choice of Amber, Amethyst, Late Dark Emerald, Royal Blue, Crystal and Carmen inserts or a rainbow of six colors. Produced from the late forties into the early sixties. Morgantown supplied Farber Bros. with Amber, Amethyst and Emerald inserts. *Suggested Value: $75-85.*

6019 Cocktail Set—(early design)—Page 106-1

Cambridge Glass Co. 1½ qt. chrome cocktail shaker with orange or walnut colored catalin handle plus six 3 oz., 4¼″ high cocktail glasses in chrome holders, on a 15½″ chrome tray. Inserts could be purchased in Amber, Amethyst, Forest Green, Royal Blue, Crystal, Carmen or a rainbow of six colors. Offered during the early forties. The 1941 wholesale price was $7.50. *Suggested Value: $75-85.*

5990 Cocktail Set—(early design)—Page 106-2
Cambridge Glass Co. 1½ qt. chrome cocktail shaker with catalin handle and trimmings plus six, 3 oz., cocktail glasses in chrome holders, on a Duchess Filigree design 16″ tray. Inserts in the following colors, Amber, Amethyst Forest Green, Royal Blue, Crystal and Carmen or a rainbow of six colors (one each of the colors offered). Circa 1941. *Suggested Value: $75-85.*

6019 Cocktail Set—(late design)—Page 107-1
Cambridge Glass Co. 1½ qt. chrome cocktail shaker with six 3 oz. cocktail glasses in chrome holders with inserts of Amber or Amethyst. Wheat border design chrome tray, 15½″ diameter. Circa 1953. *Suggested Value: $75-85.*

5775 Cocktail Set—(late design)—Page 107-2
Cambridge Glass Co. Chrome cocktail shaker: 1½ qt. capacity. Chrome cocktails with glass inserts: height 5⅜″; capacity 3 oz. Wheat border design, chrome tray: 15½″ diameter. Circa late 40's until the late 50's. Inserts of Amber, Amethyst, Late Dark Emerald, Royal Blue, Crystal and Carmen could be purchased. Six of one or a rainbow set of all six colors. *Suggested Value: $75-85.*

"Cocktail Set"—Below
Cambridge Glass Co. Chantilly pattern. Cocktail set consisting of a Chantilly etched, three piece, 32 oz. cocktail shaker, plus six, 3 oz., Chantilly etched cocktails on a 14½″ diameter chrome tray with wheat border. First offered in 1955. *Suggested Value: $175-185.*

Compotes

5565 Open Stem Compote—Page 108-1, 3

Cambridge Glass Co. Height 7½". Diameter 5½". Amber, Amethyst, Forest Green, Royal Blue and Carmen inserts were produced from 1933-1940. Most commonly found in Amethyst. Holder has only been found in chrome. *Suggested Value: $25-28. Carmen 50% more.*

5569 Compote—Page 108-2

Cambridge Glass Co./Morgantown Glass Works. Height 7½". Diameter 5½". Amber, Amethyst and Late Dark Emerald are the only colors listed in original catalogs. Due to switching and replacement of inserts other colors may be found. Farber Brothers holder offered only in chrome. Issued during the late forties, this compote was produced until 1965. Morgantown supplied inserts in Amber, Amethyst and Emerald from the late fifties until 1965. *Suggested Value: $20-22 in the colors listed.*

"Double Compote"—Page 108-4

Cambridge Glass Co. Height 5½". Inserts of Amber, Amethyst, Forest Green, Royal Blue and Carmen in chrome and silverplated Farber Bros. holders. Originally intended to hold two inserts of the same color, but also looks great with two different colored inserts. This is an early item, produced during the mid thirties and is not easily found. The silverplated version will bear the "Silvercraft" mark. *Suggested Value: Chrome $40-45. Silverplate $45-50. Carmen 50% more.*

"Candlestick Compote"—Page 108-5

Cambridge Glass Co. Height 5½". Diameter 5½". Known colors: Amber, Amethyst, Forest Green, Royal Blue, Carmen, and possibly Ebony. Farber Bros. holder/candlestick base found in chrome. The peg nappy lifts off to reveal a candleholder. Usually sold in pairs. *Suggested Value: $40-45/pair. Carmen/Ebony inserts will be priced at approximately 50% more.*

5562 High Compote—(early design)—Page 108-6, 7, 9

Cambridge Glass Co. Height 5½". Diameter 5½". Amber, Amethyst, Forest Green, Royal Blue, Carmen, Milk and Chantilly etched inserts can be found in a variety of holders, such as mosaic gold, silverplate, chrome and brass. Mosaic Gold/Silverplate circa 1933-1935. Chrome circa 1933-1942. Brass circa late fifties. One of the first items designed using the patented clip-on clip-off holder. Very easy to find in chrome. Harder in silverplate and brass. Hardest in mosaic gold. *Suggested Value: Chrome $20-25. Brass/Silverplate $25-35. Mosaic Gold $35-45. Carmen/Milk/Etched inserts in any holder valued at 50% more.*

5566 Nude Stem Compote—Page 108-8; 109-1, 3

Cambridge Glass Co. Height 7½". Diameter 5½". Inserts of Amber, Amethyst, Forest Green, Royal Blue, Carmen, Milk, Late Dark Emerald, Ebony, Diane Etched, Elaine etched and Chantilly etched have surfaced. The Chantilly etched insert has been found in both a flared and an unflared version. One of the most popular and sought after of all Farber Brothers items, this nude stem compote was produced in chrome and silverplate. The chrome version enjoyed a long period of production, lasting from approximately 1932 until 1955. Silverplated holders—due to limited production during the mid to late thirties—are much harder to find. Ebony, Milk, Elaine etched and Diane etched inserts are the most difficult to locate. *Suggested Value: Chrome $35-40. Silverplate $40-50. Etched patterns/Carmen/Ebony/Milk add 50% to the above values.*

5562 Chrome Compote—Page 109-2
7562 Brass (late design)

Cambridge Glass Co./Morgantown Glass Works. Height 5½". Diameter 5½". Amber, Amethyst, Late Dark Emerald, and Milk inserts can be found in both a chrome and a brass, pierced grape design, clip-on clip-off holder. This compote is a later issue, offered during the fifties, perhaps into the early sixties. Can be found with a thin stem as pictured or occasionally with a wider stem. This pierced grape design, piece shares its catalog number (5562) with the High Compote of earlier issue. *Suggested Value: Chrome $20-25. Brass $25-35. Carmen/Milk 50% more.*

5561 Low Compote—Page 109-4, 6

Cambridge Glass Co. Height 3½". Diameter 5½". Known colors—Amber, Amethyst, Forest Green, Royal Blue and Carmen. Possibly Ebony. This compote could be purchased from the mid to late 30's. Not listed in 1941 catalogs. To date, holder has only been found in chrome, but silverplated holders may have been made. *Suggested Value: Chrome $20-25. Carmen 50% more.*

"Sterling Compote"—Page 109-5

Cambridge Glass Co. Height 6½". Diameter 5½". This compote, produced by The Sheffield Silver Co., could be purchased with a flared or an unflared Chantilly etched insert. I have not seen this compote with any other inserts, but other etchings, such as Diane, Elaine and Rosepoint, probably do exist. *Suggested Value: $75-85.*

Condiment Sets/Oil & Vinegars

5453 Oil & Vinegar Set — Page 110-1, 7

Cambridge Glass Co./Morgantown Glass Works. 3400 line. Height of cruets 3¾". Cruet capacity 3 oz. Tray 6½" x 3¾". Chrome and silverplated holders hold inserts of Amber, Amethyst, Forest Green, Royal Blue, and Carmen. Mocha colored inserts can also be found in the Gyro-Optic pattern. Tray can have a "T", a ring, or a white plastic knob topping the handle. This set is easily found in chrome. Silverplated holders are more difficult to locate. Produced from approximately 1932 thru the early 60's in chrome and from 1932-1935 in silverplate. *Suggested Value: Chrome $30-40. Silverplate $40-45. With Carmen inserts 50% more.*

Oil & Vinegar Set — Page 110-2

Cambridge Glass Co. 3400 line. Height of cruets 5". Cruet capacity 4 oz. Tray 6½" x 3¾". Farber Brothers chrome holders hold inserts of Amber, Amethyst, Forest Green, Royal Blue and Carmen on a center handled chrome tray. (A single cruet is pictured.) *Suggested Value: $40-45. Carmen 50% more.*

5454 Condiment Set — Page 110-3, 5, 6

Cambridge Glass Co./Morgantown Glass Works. 3400 line. Consists of two 3 oz. cruets plus a salt and pepper set on a center handled tray. Dimensions: Height of cruets 3¾"; Cruet capacity 3 oz.; Height of shaker 2½". Tray 8¼" x 5½". Amber, Amethyst, Forest Green, Royal Blue, Carmen, and Late Dark Emerald inserts can be found in chrome or silver plated holders. An exceptionally good seller for Farber Brothers, this set is easily found with the exception of Carmen and Royal Blue. Trays can be found with either ring or T-shaped handles. Produced from the mid 30's into the early 60's in chrome. In silverplate, only during the mid 30's. By 1941, this set was only offered in Amber and Amethyst. Supply of these colors was maintained by Morgantown in the late 50's and early 60's. *Suggested Value: Chrome with inserts of Amber/Amethyst/Forest Green/Late Dark Emerald $40-45. Royal Blue/ Carmen $55-65. With silverplated holders, add $10 to the above values.*

"Condiment Set" — Page 110-4

Cambridge Glass Co. 3400 line. Consists of two 4 oz., upright cruets and a pair of shakers set on a T-handled or ring handled tray. Dimensions: Height of cruets 5". Cruet capacity 4 oz. Height of shakers 3½". Tray 8¼" x 5½". Amber, Amethyst, Forest Green, Royal Blue and Carmen inserts were placed in Farber Bros. chrome holders. Harder to find than the #5454 condiment set. *Suggested Value: Amber/Amethyst/Forest Green $45-55. Royal Blue/Carmen $60-70.*

Decanters/Cocktail Shakers

Decanter—Page 111-1
Cambridge Glass Co. 3400 line. Height 11¼". Capacity 24 oz. Produced only in chrome with inserts of Amber, Amethyst, Forest Green, Royal Blue, and Carmen. Produced during the mid 30's until the early 40's. This decanter is not difficult to find in Amber or Amethyst. Two different stoppers are original to this decanter as shown in both Cambridge and Farber Bros. catalogs. A faceted style or a "golf ball" type with 3400 line rays. *Suggested Value $30-35. Royal Blue/Carmen/Forest Green $50-60.*

Decanter—Page 111-2
Cambridge Glass Co. With Caprice pattern decanter: height to top of stopper is 7¼" and capacity is 35 oz. Also produced with 3400 line, 3400/92 decanter: height to top of stopper is 7½" and capacity is 32 oz. Farber Brothers Duchess Filigree design chrome holder. 3400 line inserts of Amber, Amethyst, Forest Green, Royal Blue and Carmen have been found. In the more elusive Caprice pattern, inserts of Royal Blue, Mocha, Amethyst and Forest Green have been located by collectors. This is a rare decanter, very rare with Caprice inserts. *Suggested Value: With Caprice inserts $250-300. With inserts from the 3400 line $80-85.*

Decanter—Page 111-3
Cambridge Glass Co. 3400/92. Height to top of handle 6¾". Capacity 32 oz. Chrome and mosaic gold holders were produced with inserts of Amber, Amethyst, Forest Green, Royal Blue, Late Dark Emerald, Ebony, and Carmen and Mocha in the Gyro-Optic pattern. Produced in chrome from 1932 until the late 50's. Mosaic gold was discontinued before 1940. Easily found in chrome, except with inserts of Ebony and Carmen. Mosaic gold is scarce with any color insert. Handles were either Crystal or colored to match the color of the decanter. *Suggested Value: Chrome $25-30. Mosaic Gold $45-50. With Carmen inserts $50-60. Ebony $65-75.*

Decanter—Page 111-4
Cambridge Glass Co. 3400 line. Height 10". Capacity 22 oz. Offered during the 30's through the early 40's only in chrome, with inserts of Amber, Amethyst, Forest Green, Royal Blue and Carmen, with clear applied handles. A difficult decanter to find in all colors, especially Royal Blue and Carmen. *Suggested Value: $55-65. Royal Blue/Carmen $75-85.*

Decanter — Page 111-5
Cambridge Glass Co. 3400/119. Height to top of handle 4½″. Capacity 12 oz. Amber, Amethyst, Forest Green, Royal Blue, Carmen and Ebony inserts have been found in chrome, mosaic gold and silverplated holders. Offered in chrome during the 30's and the 40's and in silverplate and mosaic gold only around 1932-1935. By 1941, only offered in Amber, Amethyst, Forest Green and Royal Blue. Harder to locate than the 32 oz. version shown, but generally priced lower. *Suggested Value: Chrome $25-30. Silverplate $30-40. Mosaic Gold $35-45. Carmen $50-60. Ebony $60-70.*

Cocktail Shaker — Page 112-1
Cambridge Glass Co. Height 11″. Capacity 3 pints. Inserts of Amber, Amethyst, Forest Green, Royal Blue and Ebony, with an applied Crystal handle. Chrome holder and lid with pouring spout. Produced from 1933 to 1940. A hard to find item, rarest in Ebony. *Suggested Value: $55-60. Ebony $85-95.*

5438 Decanter — Page 112-2, 4, 5
Cambridge Glass Co. 3400/113. Footed: 9¾″. Unfooted: 8¼″. Capacity: 35 oz. for both. Farber Brothers chrome footed or unfooted holder, with a choice of Amber, Amethyst, Forest Green, Royal Blue, Carmen and Ebony inserts. This item was produced from the mid 30's until approx. 1950. Most commonly found in Amber or Amethyst. *Suggested Value: $40-45. Carmen/Ebony $90-100.*

Decanter — Not Pictured
Cambridge Glass Co. 3400/118. Two types of this decanter exist: a footed and an unfooted version. Footed: Height 9¾″. Unfooted: 8¼″. Capacity of both: 35 oz. Amber, Amethyst, Forest Green, Royal Blue, Ebony and Carmen inserts can be found in chrome holders. Same as decanter #5438, minus the clear applied handle. This decanter has been difficult to locate with any color insert, particularly Carmen and Ebony. Produced from the mid 30's until approximately 1940. *Suggested Value: $45-50. Carmen/Ebony $95-100.*

Decanter — Page 112-3
Cambridge Glass Co. 3400 line. Height 10½″. Capacity 60 oz. 3400 ball line insert has a Farber Brothers chrome base and top. Insert has chrome spigot. Choice of Amber, Amethyst, Forest Green, Royal Blue, and Carmen. Frequently seen in Amber and Amethyst. Check for damage to the glass around the spigot and to see if the spigot is still operational. It is common for the rubber gasket around the spigot to deteriorate. This decanter was most likely offered during the mid to late thirties. *Suggested Value: $75-85.*

Decanter—Page 113-1, 2, 3

Cambridge Glass Co. Two sizes: 14 oz., height 12″; 30 oz., height 14″. Farber Brothers Duchess Filigree design holder produced only in chrome with inserts of Amber, Amethyst, Forest Green, Royal Blue and Late Dark Emerald. Offered from approximately 1941 through 1950. Difficult to find in the 30 oz. size and with Royal Blue, Forest Green or Late Dark Emerald inserts in any size. *Suggested Value: Amber/Amethyst 14 oz. $35-40. 30 oz. $55-60. Royal Blue/Forest Green/Late Dark Emerald 14 oz. $50-60. 30 oz. $75-85.*

Decanter—Page 113-4

Cambridge Glass Co. 3400/156. Height 8″. Capacity 12 oz. Inserts of Amber, Amethyst, Forest Green, Royal Blue, Carmen, Ebony and Milk can be found in chrome, brass, or silverplated holders. The chrome version of this decanter was offered from the early thirties, through the early fifties and is easily found with the exception of Carmen, Milk and Ebony. Silverplated holders were offered for a few years, from approximately 1932 to 1935. By 1950, the chrome version was only offered in Amber and Amethyst. The brass version, produced during the fifties, is difficult to locate. *Suggested Value: Chrome $25-30. Brass $45-50. Silverplate $35-40. With Milk/Carmen inserts $50-60. Ebony $70-80.*

Decanter Sets

6090 Decanter Set—Page 114-1
Cambridge Glass Co. 3400 line. Decanter: height 11¼"; capacity 24 oz. Wine: height 4⅛"; capacity 4½ oz. Tray: 14¾". This decanter set has been traced back to the early forties, but may have been produced earlier. In 1941, it was offered only in Amber and Amethyst with Farber Bros. chrome holders. Additional colors may exist. This decanter set may have also been sold with wines that were unfooted. *Suggested Value: $85-100.*

5437 Decanter Set—Page 114-2, 4
Cambridge Glass Co. Decanter 3400/113: height 9¾"; capacity 35 oz. Wine: height 5⅞"; capacity 2 oz. Chrome holders with choice of Amber, Amethyst, Forest Green, Royal Blue, Carmen or Ebony inserts. Enjoyed at least 20 years of production beginning in 1933. Glasses could be purchased to match the color of the decanter or as a rainbow set of six colors (Amber, Amethyst, Forest Green, Royal Blue, Carmen and Crystal) could be bought. If on a rectangular 19" x 12" tray, your set dates back to the 30's or 40's. If on a round 15½" tray with wheat border, it dates back to the early fifties. *Suggested Value: $95-115. Carmen/Ebony $210-$225.*

Decanter Set—Page 114-3
Cambridge Glass Co. Caprice pattern. Decanter #187: height to top of handle 7¼"; capacity 35 oz. Tumbler #188: height 2¾"; capacity 2 oz. Chrome Duchess Filigree design decanter set with inserts of Mocha, Royal Blue, Amethyst and Forest Green were originally sold with six #188 Caprice tumblers. *Suggested Value with six tumblers: $500-550. For every tumbler less than six, deduct $40.*

"Decanter Set"—Page 115-1
Cambridge Glass Co. 3400 line. Decanter: height 10½"; capacity 60 oz. Wine: 3400/92; height 2¼"; capacity 2 oz. Inserts of Amber, Amethyst, Forest Green and Royal Blue. Usually found in Amber and Amethyst in Farber Brothers chrome holders. Six 3400/92 wine glasses set on a 15" round tray complete the set. Not an easily found item. When buying check for damage to the glass around the spigot. The washer around the spigot deteriorated easily. Discontinued before 1940. *Suggested Value: $120-135.*

5852 Decanter Set—Page 115-2
Cambridge Glass Co. 3400/92. Decanter: height to top of handle 6¾"; capacity 32 oz. Wines: height 2¼"; capacity 2 oz. This set consists of a 32 oz. jug with six 2 oz. wine glasses set in patented clip-on clip-off chrome holders on a Duchess Filigree design 14" diameter tray. Offered from 1941 until 1953. In 1941, decanters with inserts of Amber or Amethyst were offered with complementary wines in a rainbow of six colors. By 1953, both the decanter and the wines were offered only in Amber and Amethyst. *Suggested Value: $65-75. Carmen/Ebony $125-145.*

5387 Decanter Set — Page 115-3

Cambridge Glass Co. 3400/92. Decanter: capacity 32 oz.; height 6¾" to the top of the handle. Wine: capacity 2 oz.; height 2¼". Offered from approximately 1932 until 1940 with inserts of Amber, Amethyst, Forest Green, Royal Blue, Carmen and Ebony set in chrome Farber Brothers holders on a 16½" x 9" rectangular tray. This set could be purchased for $12.50 in 1935. *Suggested Value: $65-75. Carmen/Ebony $125-145.*

5466 Decanter Set — Page 116-1

Cambridge Glass Co. Decanter 3400/92: height to top of handle 6¾"; capacity 32 oz. Cordials: height 4¼"; capacity 1 oz. Tray: 14" x 12". Offered from approximately 1933 until 1940 with inserts of Amber, Amethyst, Forest Green, Royal Blue, Carmen and Ebony in chrome holders. Ebony is the most difficult color to find. *Suggested Value: $95-115 complete with eight cordials. Carmen $125-150 Ebony $175-200.*

Decanter Set — Page 116-2

Cambridge Glass Co. 3400/92: height to top of handle 6¾"; capacity 32 oz. Wine: height 2¼"; capacity 2 oz. This decanter set in mosaic gold dates back to 1932 and was discontinued prior to 1940. Originally, this set was comprised of a tilted decanter with six wines on a ring handled tray. Amber, Amethyst, Forest Green, Royal Blue, Carmen and Ebony are the inserts that can be located. A difficult set to find in mosaic gold with inserts of any color. Also produced in chrome during the same time period. *Suggested Value: Chrome $75-85. Carmen/ Ebony $125-150. Mosaic Gold holders will add $40 to the above values.*

5853 Decanter Set — Page 116-3

Cambridge Glass Co. 3400 line. Decanter: height 11¼"; capacity 24 oz. Cordials: height 4¼"; capacity 1 oz. Duchess Filigree design 14" tray. Amber or Amethyst decanters with six cordials to match decanter or a rainbow set of six colors. Chrome only. Circa 1941. *Suggested Value: $80-95.*

Tantalus Set — Page 117-1

Cambridge Glass Co. Decanter 3400/156. Height 8". Capacity 12 oz. Overall dimensions: 12½" x 4" x 10½". This novel decanter set contains three different colored decanters, one each of Amber, Forest Green and Royal Blue, all with chrome holders. Chrome carrier with black composition handle has locking device. Offered during the mid to late thirties. *Suggested Value: $100-$110.*

Decanter Set—Page 117-2

Cambridge Glass Co. Decanter 3400 line: height 11¼"; capacity 24 oz. Cordials #1900: height 2"; capacity 1 oz. Amber and Amethyst inserts in Farber Brothers chrome holders set on a 14", Duchess Filigree design, chrome tray, Circa early 1940's. *Suggested Value: $75-85.*

5555 Tantalus Set—Page 117-3

Cambridge Glass Co. Decanter 3400/156. Height 8". Capacity 12 oz. Height overall 10¾". Length 13". Width 4". Three different colored decanters in chrome holders, (usually Amber, Forest Green and Royal Blue) set in a chrome carrier that comes complete with a locking device. Could also be purchased minus the chrome holders on the decanters. In 1935, this set could be purchased for $14.50 at jewelry, gift and better department stores. Discontinued prior to 1941. *Suggested Value: $100-110.*

5482 Tantalus Set—Below

A third tantalus set also exists. Three 3400/156 decanters, all in chrome holders in a handled chrome holder, not under lock and key. This tantalus set proves to be more difficult to locate than ones under lock and key. As with the other Tantalus sets, the #5482 set was sold during the mid to late thirties and discontinued before 1941. *Suggested Value: $110-120.*

5482

Ice Pails/Ice Tubs

5407 Ice Pail—Page 118-1

Cambridge Glass Co. Tally-Ho Pattern. Height 10". Diameter 5". Amber, Amethyst, Forest Green, Royal Blue, Carmen and Ebony inserts can be found in chrome Farber Bros. holders. Originally sold with ice tongs, this ice pail was first sold in 1933. Dropped from production by 1941, but has proven easy to find with the exception of Carmen and Ebony. In 1933, with $7.50, you could purchase this ice pail. *Suggested Value: $45-55. Carmen/Ebony $85-95.*

5441 Ice Tub—Page 118-2

Cambridge Glass Co. 3400 line. Height 4½". Diameter 9". Amber, Amethyst, Forest Green, Royal Blue, Carmen and possibly Ebony inserts can be found in chrome. Came complete with ice tongs. Produced only during the mid to late 30's. Harder to find than the 5407 Ice Pail. *Suggested Value: $50-60. Carmen/Ebony $85-95.*

Ice Tub—Page 118-3

Cambridge Glass Co. Height 5¼". Diameter 7" handle to handle. Chantilly etching on Pristine blank set on an unmarked Farber Brothers chrome base. This ice tub can also be found with an identical sterling base, produced and marketed by the Sheffield Silver Co. Difficult to find in chrome. Ice tubs with sterling bases seem to be more plentiful. *Suggested Value: $75-85. Sterling $80-90.*

Mustards/Marmalades/Mayonnaises

6121 Marmalade or Jam Jar — Page 119-1
Cambridge Glass Co./Morgantown Glass Works. Height 5". Amber, Amethyst, Late Dark Emerald and Milk inserts were set in chrome or brass Farber Bros. holders. Offered during the late forties until the early sixties. Morgantown produced inserts in Amber, Emerald, Milk and Amethyst. Easily found in chrome. Brass is more difficult to find. *Suggested Value: Chrome $18-22. Brass $35-40.*

"Footed Marmalade" — Page 119-2
Cambridge Glass Co. Height 5¼" or 5½". Inserts of Amber, Amethyst, Forest Green, Royal Blue, and possibly Carmen. Holders can be found in chrome or mosaic gold. Note the two, slightly different bases, on the items pictured, hence the difference in height. Offered during the mid to late thirties. Difficult to find in mosaic gold. *Suggested Value: Chrome $18-25. Mosaic Gold $35-40.*

"Raised Marmalade" — Page 119-3
Cambridge Glass Co. Height 5". Diameter of tray 10¼". Chrome and silverplated holders with inserts of Amber, Amethyst, Forest Green, Royal Blue and Carmen. May have been offered by Farber Bros. during the late thirties into the early forties. *Suggested Value: Chrome $25-30. Silverplate $30-35.*

"Mayonnaise" — Page 119-4
Cambridge Glass Co. Height 4¼". Diameter 3½". This Farber Brothers chrome holder with Crystal insert was produced during the late forties. *Suggested Value: $18-22.*

"Mustard" — Page 119-5
Cambridge Glass Co. Height 4½". Inserts of Amber, Amethyst, Forest Green, and Royal Blue can be found set into chrome, mosaic gold or silverplated Farber Bros. holders. Easily found in chrome. Silverplate and mosaic gold prove more difficult to locate. Chrome holders circa 1932-1940. Silverplated and mosaic gold holders circa 1932-1935. *Suggested Value: Chrome $15-$20. Silverplate $18-22.*

5926 Marmalade Jar — Page 119-6
Cambridge Glass Co. Dimensions: 7½" x 4¼". Crystal insert with cut "floral design" or Chantilly etching can be found in a Duchess Filigree chrome design holder with chrome lid and finial. Produced during the early fifties. Similar items were offered during the late 30's and early 40's, with the same item number, but without the "floral design" cut into the insert and with either a glass or an orange colored catalin knob on the lid. *Suggested Value: $18-22. Chantilly etched $45-50.*

5526 Marmalade Jar—Page 119-7

Cambridge Glass Co. Height 4½". Choice of Amber, Amethyst, Royal Blue and Forest Green inserts. Forest Green no longer listed in 1941 company catalogs. Also found with a Gyro-Optic insert in Mocha. Only chrome and silverplated holders have been found, but I suspect you may find this marmalade in mosaic gold also. Offered by Farber Bros. in chrome, from the mid thirties until the early forties, and in silverplate from approximately 1932 to 1935. Easily found in chrome. *Suggested Value: Chrome $15-20. Silverplate $18-22. Mosaic Gold $25-30.*

Pitchers

6124 Pitcher—Page 120-1, 4
Cambridge Glass Co. 3400 line. Height 8½″. Capacity 76 oz. Pitchers of Amber, Amethyst and Late Dark Emerald set in chrome Farber Brothers bases. May have also been produced in Royal Blue, although a catalog from 1953, does not list that color. Offered during the early fifties, this pitcher was a good seller for Farber Brothers. *Suggested Value: $50-60.*

6123 Juice Jug—Not Pictured—Similar to 6124
Cambridge Glass Co. 3400 line. Height 5¾″. Capacity 22 oz. Amber, Amethyst and Late Dark Emerald pitchers set on chrome Farber Bros. bases. May also be found in Royal Blue, although this color is not listed in original catalogs. Offered during the early fifties. Did not sell as well as the larger size, making it harder to find. *Suggested Value: $40-45.*

Pitcher—Page 120-2
Cambridge Glass Co. 3400 line. Height 9¾″. Capacity 48 oz. Known colors: Amber, Amethyst, Forest Green, Royal Blue. Farber Brothers chrome holder and pouring spout. From all indications, this pitcher was produced before 1940, and today, is difficult to find. *Suggested Value: $65-75.*

Pitcher—Page 120-3
Cambridge Glass Co. 3400 line. Height 9″. Capacity 48 oz. Known colors: Amber, Amethyst, Forest Green and Royal Blue. Holder produced in chrome. Due to a short period of production, during the mid to late thirties, this pitcher is hard to locate. Has been spotted in Amber more often than any other color. *Suggested Value: $60-70.*

6131 Pitcher—Page 120-5
Cambridge Glass Co. 3400 line. Height 7½″. Capacity 76 oz. Available in Amber, Amethyst, Late Dark Emerald, or Milk with chrome or brass holders. Due to a limited production, the brass version of this pitcher, can be difficult to find. Produced during the early to late 50's. *Suggested Value: Chrome $50-55. Brass $60-70.*

Pitcher—Page 120-6, 8
Cambridge Glass Co. 3400/114. Height 8½″. Capacity 64 oz. Also produced using similar insert from the Gyro-Optic line. Inserts of Amber, Amethyst, Forest Green, Royal Blue, Carmen, Mocha and possibly Ebony were placed in Farber Brothers chrome and silverplated holders. Chrome holders were produced during the years of 1933-1940 and are easily found. Silverplated holders were produced circa 1932-1935 and are much more difficult to find. *Suggested Value: Chrome $50-60. Silverplate $55-65. With inserts of Carmen/Ebony $85-95.*

6130 Juice Jug—Page 120-7

Cambridge Glass Co. 3400 line. Height 5″. Capacity 22 oz. Farber Bros. chrome or brass holders, with Amber, Amethyst, Late Dark Emerald or Milk inserts, were available during the early to late fifties. *Suggested Value: Chrome $40-45. Brass $50-60.*

Pitcher Sets

5442 Claret or Punch Set—Page 121-1

Cambridge Glass Co. Pitcher 3400 line: height 9″; capacity 48 oz. Tumbler: height 3½″; capacity 6 oz. First offered by Farber Brothers in 1932, this set was discontinued before 1940. Inserts of Amber, Amethyst, Forest Green, and Royal Blue could be purchased. Not an easy set to find. *Suggested Value: $130-140.*

"Pitcher Set"—Page 121-2; 122-2

Cambridge Glass Co. Pitcher 3400 line: height 7½″; capacity 76 oz. Tumbler: height 5″; capacity 12 oz. Farber Brothers took their #6131 pitcher and added six of the #5633 tumblers to form this easily found pitcher set. Holders made from chrome or brass hold inserts of Amber, Amethyst, Late Dark Emerald, and Milk inserts. Both offered during the fifties, the brass version of this set is much more difficult to find than chrome. *Suggested Value: Chrome $115-130. Brass $175-200.*

5389 Beer or Water Set—Page 122-1

Cambridge Glass Co. Pitcher 3400/114: height 8½″; capacity 64 oz. Tumbler 3400/112: capacity 8 oz. Choice of Amber, Amethyst, Forest Green, Royal Blue, Carmen, and Ebony in chrome and silverplated holders. Also produced with Mocha inserts from the Gyro-Optic line. Offered from approximately 1932-1940 in chrome and from 1932-1935 in silverplate. Three different size trays are original to this set. A 14″ diameter, round tray, a 19″ x 16″ rectangular tray, and a 12″ x 14″ rectangular tray. Most difficult to find in Carmen and Ebony. This set had a suggested retail price of $22.50, in 1934. *Suggested Value: Chrome $125-135. Silverplate $135-145. With inserts of Ebony/Carmen $195-200.*

Relishes/Preserve Dishes/
Pickle Dishes/Buffet Pieces

"Relish"—Page 123-1
Cambridge Glass Co. 3500 line with #1900, 1 oz. tumbler. Height 3″. Diameter 5½″. Found with inserts of Amber, Amethyst, Forest Green, Crystal, and Royal Blue in chrome holders. *Suggested Value: $25-30.*

6113 Lazy Susan/Centerpiece—Page 123-2
Cambridge Glass Co. Height 8″. Spread 12″. Produced in Amber, Amethyst, Late Dark Emerald and Royal Blue but found primarily in Amber and Amethyst. Called a lazy susan in advertisements from the forties and in fifties ads, a center piece. Chrome Farber Brothers peg nappies and removable candlestick base. Not an easy Farber Brothers item to locate, but practical even today. *Suggested Value: $90-100.*

Be aware that a second lazy susan/centerpiece exists. Produced in chrome with the same choice of inserts, it has a removable Duchess Filigree design 14″ tray for a base instead of a removable candlestick base. *Suggested Value: $95-105.*

"Relish"—Page 123-3
Cambridge Glass Co. Height 2″. Diameter 5½″. Crystal and Royal Blue inserts can be found in both chrome and brass Farber Brothers holders. *Suggested Value: Chrome $25-35. Brass $35-40.*

5783 Relish—Page 123-4
Cambridge Glass Co. 3500/68. Diameter 5½″. Height 3″. Amber, Amethyst, Late Dark Emerald and Crystal inserts can be found in chrome Farber Brothers bases. A brass version was offered only with Crystal glass. Both chrome and brass were offered during the 50's. Easily found in all colors except Crystal. *Suggested Value: Chrome $10-12. Brass $12-15.*

5784 Relish—Page 123-5, 10
Cambridge Glass Co. 3500/70. 4 part. Diameter 7½″. Height 3″. Amber, Amethyst, Late Dark Emerald and Crystal inserts can be found on chrome Farber Brothers bases. A brass version was offered only with Crystal glass. Both chrome and brass were offered during the 50's. Easily found in all colors except Crystal. *Suggested Value: Chrome $15-18. Brass $16-20.*

5782 Relish—Page 123-6, 8, 12
Cambridge Glass Co. 3500/69. 3 part. Diameter 6½″. Height 3″. Amber, Amethyst, Late Dark Emerald and Crystal inserts can be found on chrome Farber Brothers bases. A brass version was offered only with Crystal glass. Both chrome and brass were offered during the 50's. Easily found in all colors except Crystal. *Suggested Value: Chrome $12-15. Brass $15-18.*

6111 Silent Butler—Page 123-7, 9
Cambridge Glass Co. Height 3″. Diameter 5½″, exclusive of handle. Amber, Amethyst, Forest Green and Royal Blue are the colors that have been found. Due to replacement of inserts, other colors such as Carmen and Milk may surface. This chrome Farber Brothers silent butler has a hinged cover and walnut handle. Although produced during the early fifties, it proves to be a somewhat difficult item to find. Note that Farber Bros. produced several different style silent butlers in chrome, brass and copper that did not make use of inserts of any kind. *Suggested Value: $50-60.*

"Preserve Dish"—Page 123-11
Cambridge Glass Co. 3500 line. Height to top of handle 5¾″. Diameter, excluding handle, 5¼″. Found only in chrome, with inserts of Amber, Amethyst, Forest Green, Royal Blue and Crystal. Offered during the 40's. *Suggested Value: $18-22.*

5781 Preserve Dish—Page 124-1
Cambridge Glass Co. 3500/131. Dimensions: 6¾″ x 4¾″. Height overall 4¾″. Chrome holder with overhead spoon. Choice of Amber, Amethyst, Forest Green, Royal Blue, Crystal and Chantilly etched inserts. Offered during the 40's. An easily found item except with etched inserts. *Suggested Value: $15-18. With etched inserts, double the price.*

"Double Oval Shaped Relish"—Page 124-2
Cambridge Glass Co. 3500 line. Height 7″. Diameter 11″. Chrome only, with inserts of Amber, Amethyst, Forest Green, Royal Blue and Crystal. Swivel base allows for easy serving. Circa 40's. Difficult to find. *Suggested Value: $30-35.*

"Relish/Preserve Dish"—Page 124-3
Cambridge Glass Co. 3500 line. Height to top of handles 4″. Diameter, excluding handles, 5¼″. Choice of Amber, Amethyst, Forest Green, Royal Blue and Crystal inserts in Farber Brothers chrome holders. Produced during the 40's. *Suggested Value: $18-22.*

5910 Double Relish—Page 124-4
Cambridge Glass Co. 3500/129. Dimensions: 13¾″ x 5½″; height overall 5½″. Amber, Amethyst, Forest Green, Royal Blue or Crystal inserts. Farber Brothers holder, with center handle, holds both a spoon and a fork. Produced during the early 40's. *Suggested Value: $25-30.*

5915 Relish/Preserve Dish—Page 124-5
Cambridge Glass Co. 3500 Gadroon line. Dimenions: length 11″; width 4¼″. Duchess Filigree design handled tray in chrome holds a 2-part, divided, Crystal insert. Offered by Farber Brothers from approximately 1940 through the late 50's, in Crystal only, but be aware that other colors may exist, due to replacement of inserts. An easily found item. *Suggested Value: Crystal $15-18.*

"Covered Relish"—Page 124-6

Cambridge Glass Co. 3500 Gadroon line. Dimensions: 11″ x 4¼″ x 3″. Duchess Filigree design, handled, chrome tray with chrome lid, holds a two part insert in Amber, Amethyst, Forest Green, Royal Blue or Crystal. Circa 1940's. *Suggested Value: $20-25.*

Relish/Preserve Dish"—Page 124-7

Cambridge Glass Co. 3500 line. Height to top of handle 6″. Diameter, excluding handle, 5¼″. Produced during the 40's in chrome only, with inserts of Amber, Amethyst, Forest Green, Royal Blue and Crystal. *Suggested Value: $18-22.*

"Toothpick"—Page 124-8

Cambridge Glass Co. #1900. Height 3½″. Length 6¾″. I am taking a guess as to the original use of this piece, since no references have been found in Farber Brothers catalogs. Choice of Amber, Amethyst, Forest Green, Royal Blue, Crystal and Carmen inserts in a chrome holder with underplate. *Suggested Value: $18-20.*

5778 Preserve Dish—Page 124-9

Cambridge Glass Co. 3500/129. Dimensions: 5½″ x 5½″. Height overall 4½″. Amber, Amethyst, Forest Green, Royal Blue, Crystal and Elaine etched, are the inserts you can encounter. Farber Brothers chrome holder with raised tulip design in each corner. Came complete with a chromium plated spoon. Offered during the 1940's. *Suggested Value: $15-18. With etched inserts, double the price.*

5776 Pickle Dish—Page 124-10

Cambridge Glass Co. 3500/129. Dimensions: 5½″ x 5½″. Height overall 4½″. Holders found only in chrome, with inserts of Amber, Amethyst, Forest Green, Royal Blue, Crystal and Elaine etched. Holder has raised tulip design at each corner. Produced during the 1940's. Difficult to find with etched inserts. *Suggested Value: $15-18. With etched inserts, double the price.*

5779 Pickle Dish—Page 124-11

Cambridge Glass Co. 3500/131. Dimensions: 6¾″ x 4¾″. Height overall 4¾″. Made during the 40's, only in chrome, with inserts of Amber, Amethyst, Forest Green, Royal Blue, Crystal and Chantilly etched. Came complete with a serving fork. *Suggested Value: $15-18. With etched inserts, double the price.*

Salts and Peppers

5874 Salt & Pepper Set — Page 125-1, 6
5875 with tray
Cambridge Glass Co./Morgantown Glass Works. 3400 line. Height 3½". Tray dimensions: 6½" x 3¾". Amber, Amethyst, Forest Green, Royal Blue, Late Dark Emerald, Milk and Chantilly etched are the inserts found to date. Chrome, brass, mosaic gold by Farber Bros. and sterling silver by The Sheffield Silver Co. are the holders you can find. Silverplate may have been made. Also produced, an unhandled version in the same colors and materials as shown. Offered during the forties and into the late fifties. Easiest to find in Amethyst and Amber. Morgantown provided only Amber, Amethyst and Milk inserts during the late fifties — these colors were also supplied by Cambridge earlier. *Suggested Value (both handled and unhandled): Chrome $20-25. Brass $35-45. Mosaic Gold $35-45. Sterling $40-45. If tray is included, add $5-8.*

5712 Salt & Pepper Set — Page 125-2, 4
5711 with tray
Cambridge Glass Co. 3400 line. Height 3½". Tray Dimensions: 6½" x 3¾". Amber, Amethyst, Forest Green, Royal Blue and Carmen inserts can be found in chrome holders. Produced during the late thirties into the early forties. These shakers are slightly difficult to find. *Suggested Value: $25-30. Carmen inserts add 50% to above price. If tray included, add $5-8.*

5450 Salt & Pepper Set — Page 125-3, 5, 7, 9
5451 with tray
Cambridge Glass Co./Morgantown Glass Works. 3400 line. Height 2½". Tray Dimensions: 6½" x 3¾". Offered in several different colors: Amber, Amethyst, Forest Green, Late Dark Emerald, Royal Blue, Carmen, Chantilly etched, Rosepoint etched, Pistachio, Dianthus Pink and Crystal. Holders can be found in chrome (most common), mosaic gold, silverplate and sterling. Sterling holders were produced by The Sheffield Silver Co. One of the original items offered using the patented clip-on clip-off holder, by 1941 these shakers were offered only in chrome, with inserts of Amber, Amethyst, Forest Green and Royal Blue. Produced for approximately thirty years, these shakers are easily found in chrome. Mosaic gold, sterling and silverplated holders may take a little searching. Inserts of Pistachio, Dianthus Pink, and all of the etched patterns are priced to reflect their scarcity. These shakers can be found with both Crystal applied handles and handles that match the color of the shaker. Morgantown produced Amethyst, Amber and Emerald inserts during the late fifties and early sixties. *Suggested Value: Chrome $18-22. Silverplate $20-25. Mosaic Gold/Sterling $30-35. Dianthus Pink/Pistachio/etched inserts add 50% to the above prices. If tray is included, add $5-8.*

5710 Salt & Pepper Set—Page 125-8, 10
5713 with tray
Cambridge Glass Co. 3400 line. Height 4½". Tray Dimensions: 6½" x 3¾". Offered in a 1941 catalog in Amber, Amethyst, Forest Green, Royal Blue and Carmen with chrome holders. I have not seen these shakers in holders besides chrome. Probably produced from the late 30's into the early forties. In 1941, these shakers had a wholesale price of $1.65 per pair with tray, $1.15 without. *Suggested Value: $30-35. Carmen inserts add 50% more to above price. If tray is included, add $5-8.*

"Open Salt"—Page 125-11
Cambridge Glass Co. Nautilus pattern. Height 1¾". Length overall 2¼". Amber, Amethyst, Royal Blue, Forest Green, and Carmen inserts in chrome Farber Brothers holders. Difficult to find in any color due to a short period of production during the mid to late thirties. May have originally been sold in sets. *Suggested Value: $30-35 each.*

Sugar & Creamers

5455 Sugar & Creamer Set—Page 126-1
Cambridge Glass Co. Creamer 3400 line. Sugar no catalog reference. Height of sugar 4″. Height of creamer 4¼″. From approximately 1932 until 1941, this set could be purchased with Amber, Amethyst, Forest Green, Royal Blue, and Chantilly etched inserts in chrome or silverplated holders, with sugar tongs on a 10″ x 5″, T-handled tray. In 1941, the same set, catalog number 5455 ½, could still be purchased in chrome, but by then Forest Green was no longer offered and the set rested on a rectangular 10″ x 5″ tray. In 1941, the sugar and creamer also could be purchased individually. Catalog number for the sugar was 5527 and 5528 was the number for the creamer. *Suggested Value: Chrome $30-40/set. Silverplate $35-45/set. Chantilly etched $50-60/set.*

5527 Sugar: Chrome $15-18. Silverplate $18-20. Chantilly etched $22-25.

5528 Creamer: Chrome $15-18. Silverplate $18-20. Chantilly etched $22-25.

5456 Sugar & Creamer Set—Page 126-2, 3, 6, 8
5456X without tray
Cambridge Glass Co./Morgantown Glass Works. 3400 line. Height of sugar with lid 4″. Height of creamer 3″. Tray dimensions: 10″ x 5″. Amber, Amethyst, Forest Green and Chantilly etched inserts can be found in chrome or brass Farber Brothers holders. Offered during the late forties into the late fifties. Relatively easy to find, except in Chantilly etched. Morgantown supplied Amethyst, Amber, Milk and Emerald inserts only. *Suggested Value: Chrome $30-35. Brass $45-50. Chantilly etched $45-55. Deduct $5 if without tray.*

Sugar & Creamer Set—Page 126-4, 5, 10, 11
Cambridge Glass Co. Creamer 3400 line. Sugar no catalog reference. Height of sugar 3″. Height of creamer 4¼″. Found in Amber, Amethyst, Forest Green, Chantilly etched and Royal Blue. Amber is the most common color found. Offered in chrome and mosaic chrome during the late 40's. The mosaic chrome set pictured has an unslotted sugar lid which is not normally found in these sets. *Suggested Value: Chrome $25-35. Chantilly etched $45-55. Mosaic Chrome $65-75 with any insert.*

Sugar & Creamer Set—Page 126-7, 9
Cambridge Glass Co. 3400/98. Height of sugar 5″. Height of creamer 5″. Produced during the early to mid thirties, this sugar and creamer set was no longer offered by 1940. Found in Amber, Amethyst, Forest Green, Royal Blue, Carmen, Ebony and Heatherbloom in chrome holders. Holders will frequently be found split or cracked. A difficult set to find in any color. Originally sold on chrome 10″ x 5″ rectangular tray with or without a T-shaped center holder. *Suggested Value: $45-55. Ebony/Carmen/Heatherbloom $65-75.*

Vases

Vase—Page 127-1
Cambridge Glass Co. Caprice Pattern #337. Height 4½". Amethyst, Forest Green, Mocha and Royal Blue inserts can be found in chrome Farber Brothers clip-on clip-off holders. A difficult item to find in any color. *Suggested Value: $75-85.*

Vase—Page 127-3
Cambridge Glass Co. Height 10¼". Royal Blue insert with mosaic gold Farber Brothers holder. This rare and unusual item was offered after 1932 and discontinued before 1940. Possibly produced with chrome holders and inserts of other colors. *Suggested Value: $75-85.*

A last minute addition—Too late for photographing but definitely worth mentioning is an ivy ball which was recently added to my collection. It contains a 5½" Cambridge 3400/93 insert encased by a Farber Bros. chrome clip-on clip-off holder. Expect to find inserts in Amber, Amethyst, Forest Green, Royal Blue and possibly Carmen and Ebony. It is an early item which dates back to 1932. *Suggested Value: $60-70.*

Miscellaneous

"Bitters Bottle"—Page 127-2
Cambridge Glass Co. 3400 line. Capacity 4 oz. Height 5¼". Amber, Amethyst, Forest Green, and Royal Blue inserts, in Farber Brothers chrome holders. Produced during the mid to late 30's. The cork that surrounds the top is difficult to find in good condition. *Suggested Value: $30-35.*

Cigarette Urn—Page 127-4
Cambridge Glass Co. Chantilly pattern. Height 3". Diameter 3". Sterling clip-on clip-off holder, produced and marketed by The Sheffield Silver Company, holds a Chantilly etched insert. Other etchings may be found. *Suggested Value: $35-40.*

"Bowl"—Page 127-5
Cambridge Glass Co. Height 3¾". Diameter 7¼". Farber Brothers chrome base with Ebony bowl is the only combination that has surfaced. It is possible that other colors exist. Bowl bears the ⚠ trademark. Offered during the mid to late thirties. *Suggested Value: $40-45.*

5563 Handled Basket—Page 127-6
Cambridge Glass Co. Height 5½". Diameter 5½". Amber, Amethyst, Forest Green, Royal Blue and Carmen inserts in silverplate or chrome holders. Approximate years of production—1933 into the mid 40's. Silverplate is harder to locate since only offered during the 30's. In 1941, the wholesale price of this basket was only $1.35, with the exception of Carmen which sold for $1.55. *Suggested Value: Chrome $20-25. Silverplate $25-30. With inserts of Carmen, add 50% to the above prices.*

5654 Cheese & Cracker Dish—Page 127-7
Cambridge Glass Co. Diameter 10". Duchess Filigree design plate with 5" Crystal butterdish with "floral design" cut into the cover. Available during the late 30's into the early 50's in Crystal only. *Suggested Value: $20-25.*

Corning

Serve your favorite recipes in these casseroles, pie plates, and beefsteak and vegetable dishes designed by Farber Brothers using Pyrex™ inserts from The Corning Glass Works. Casserole, vegetable dish, pie plate and beefsteak dish inserts, crystal in color, were supplied by Corning from approximately 1920 until as late as 1965. The shape and style of these inserts changed gradually throughout the years. The changes can be seen on the following pages.

Many casseroles came with designs engraved on the covers. Until 1921, these designs were likely done by J.Hoare & Company, an engraving firm, housed in the same building as Corning. In 1921, after J.Hoare & Co. closed, Corning began its own engraving, but ceased in 1926 because of low profits. From 1932 to 1941, engraving Pyrex™ brand bakingware was again offered by Corning and sold to numerous metalcraft companies.

During the twenties and thirties, Farber Brothers purchased engraved Pyrex™ inserts and placed them in both nickelplated and silverplated holders. Each casserole, vegetable dish and pie plate produced could be purchased in nickelplate as well as silverplate. By 1932, the same items could be purchased in chromium plated holders. Many of the same holders that were once made in silverplate and nickelplate were discontinued and reoffered in chrome. New styles were also designed such as casseroles made from one piece or metal with no soldering or welding of any kind and casseroles in which the Pyrex™ inserts were simply placed on Farber Brothers chromium plated trays. For thirty years these casseroles, vegetable dishes and pie plates in chromium plated Farber Brothers holders could be found in jewelry, gift and department stores. Many brides-to-be were given these Farber Brothers items and it is not surprising that so many are still in use today. They are as useful now as they were when they were first made. Imagine you can still purchase similar casseroles and pie plate inserts to replace ones accidentally broken or to set in that lonely Farber Brothers holder found at the flea market last weekend.

During the early sixties, chrome, brass and copper, 2 and 3 quart ice buckets using Pyrex™ liners were offered for sale. These were the last, in a long line of Pyrex™ based products, to be introduced by Farber Brothers.

On the following pages is an assortment of the Farber Brothers items produced using Corning inserts. *Suggested Value for all casseroles and beefsteak dishes is $18-20, ice buckets $20-35, pie plates $12-15 and vegetable dishes $15-18.*

5800 Chrome
7800 Brass
8800 Copper Ice Tub—Page 128-1
Corning Glass Works. 2 quart capacity. This ice tub was offered during the early sixties in chrome, brass or copper in 2 and 3 quart sizes. The solid brass tub pictured, features a plastic wrapped handle and brass lid topped with an orange catalin knob. *Suggested Value: Chrome $20-25. Brass $25-30. Copper $30-35.*

No. 1424-S
7″ Round ....Capacity 1 qt.
No. 1425-S
8″ Round ....Capacity 1½ qt.

No. 1426-S
8 x 6″ Oval ....Capacity 1 qt.
No. 1427-S
9 x 7″ Oval ....Capacity 2 qt.

No. 1400-S
7″ Round ....Capacity 1 qt.
No. 1401-S
8″ Round ....Capacity 1½ qt.

No. 1428-S
7″ Round ....Capacity 1 qt.
No. 1429-S
8″ Round ....Capacity 1½ qt.

No. 1402-S
8 x 6″ Oval ....Capacity 1 qt.
No. 1403-S
9 x 7″ Oval ....Capacity 2 qt.

No. 1430-S
8 x 6″ Oval ....Capacity 1 qt.
No. 1431-S
9 x 7″ Oval ....Capacity 2 qt.

Circa 1920

No. 1443-S
7" Round ....Capacity 1 qt.

No. 1444-S
8" Round ....Capacity 1½ qt.

No. 1445-S
8 x 6" Oval ....,...Capacity 1 qt.

No. 1446-S
9 x 7" Oval ....Capacity 2 qt.

No. 1408-S
7" Round ....Capacity 1 qt.

No. 1409-S
8" Round ....Capacity 1½ qt.

No. 530-S
7" Round ....Capacity 1 qt.

No. 531-S
8" Round ....Capacity 1½ qt.

No. 1410-S
8 x 6" Oval ....Capacity 1 qt.

No. 1411-S
9 x 7" Oval . ...Capacity 2 qt.

Circa 1920

No. 1443-N
7″ Round ....Capacity 1 qt.

No. 1444-N
8″ Round ....Capacity 1½ qt.

No. 1445-N
8 x 6″ Oval ....Capacity 1 qt.

No. 1446-N
9 x 7″ Oval ....Capacity 2 qt.

No. 1408-N
7″ Round ....Capacity 1 qt.

No. 1409-N
8″ Round ....Capacity 1½ qt.

No. 1410-N
8 x 6″ Oval ....Capacity 1 qt.

No. 1411-N
9 x 7″ Oval ....Capacity 2 qt.

No. 530-N
7″ Round ....Capacity 1 qt.

No. 531-N
8″ Round ....Capacity 1½ qt.

No. 532-N
8 x 6″ Oval .... .Capacity 1 qt.

υ. 533-N
9 x 7″ Oval ....·....Capacity 2 qt.

Circa 1920

No. 1424-N
7" Round ....Capacity 1 qt.

No. 1425-N
8" Round ....Capacity 1½ qt.

No. 1426-N
8 x 6" Oval ....Capacity 1 qt.

No. 1427-N
9 x 7" Oval ....Capacity 2 qt.

No. 1400-N
7" Round ....Capacity 1 qt.

No. 1401-N
8" Round ....Capacity 1½ qt.

No. 1402-N
8 x 6" Oval ....Capacity 1 qt.

No. 1403-N
9 x 7" Oval ....Capacity 2 qt.

No. 1428-N
7" Round ....Capacity 1 qt.

No. 1429-N
8" Round ....Capacity 1½ qt.

No. 1430-N
8 x 6" Oval ....Capacity 1 qt.

No. 1431-N
9 x 7" Oval ....Capacity 2 qt.

Circa 1920

NICKEL PLATED CASSEROLES—PYREX LININGS
All frames are seamless and sold separately if desired

No. 15-N
7" Round ....Capacity 1 qt.

No. 17-N
8" Round ....Capacity 1½ qt.

No. 19-N
8 x 6" Oval ....Capacity 1 qt.

No. 21-N
9 x 7" Oval ....Capacity 2 qt.

No. 1447-N
8" Square ....Capacity 1½ qt.

No. 1436-N
7" Round ....Capacity 1 qt.

No. 1437-N
8" Round ....Capacity 1½ qt.

BEEFSTEAK DISHES—PYREX LININGS
All frames are seamless and sold separately if desired

No. 1420-N
9 x 6" Oval ....Capacity 1 qt.

No. 1421-N
10 x 7" Oval ....Capacity 1½ qt.

No. 1422-N
9 x 6" Oval ....Capacity 1 qt.

No. 1423-N
10 x 7" Oval ....Capacity 1½ qt.

Circa 1920

NICKEL PLATED PIE PLATES--PYREX LININGS

All frames are seamless and sold separately if desired

No. 1414-N—8"
No. 1415-N—9"

No. 1416-N—8"
No. 1417-N—19"

No. 1418-N—8"
No. 1419-N—9"

No. 1432-N—8"
No. 1433-N—9"

NICKEL PLATED VEGETABLE DISHES

No. 1448-N   Covered Baking Dish
                      2 Pieces
10 x 7"—Oval

No. 1449-N   Double Compartment
9"—Round

Circa 1920

SILVER PLATED PIE PLATES—PYREX LININGS

All frames are seamless and sold separately if desired

Plain or Hammered Frame
No. 1932—8"
No. 1933—9"

No. 1414—8"
No. 1415—9"

No. 1416—8"
No. 1417—9"

No. 1418—8"
No. 1419—9"

BEEFSTEAK DISHES—PYREX LININGS

No. 1420—Oval 9" x 6½"   Capacity 1 qt.
No. 1421—Oval 10½" x 7¾"   Capacity 1½ qts.

No. 1422—Oval 9" x 6"   Capacity 1 qt.
No. 1423—Oval 10½" x 7¾"   Capacity 1½ qts.

Circa 1920

5996

5810

6052
6053

6050
6051

5225

Circa 1941

75

5901 CASSEROLE
9 in. round Pyrex glass liner on beautiful Duchess filigree design pierced plate. Diameter 12 in. Capacity 2 qts.

5021 CASSEROLE
8 in. round glass liner in lustrous chromium frame. A practical and beautiful item for the table! Capacity 1 ½ qts.

6021 CASSEROLE
8 in. round Pyrex liner in lustrous chrome frame. Capacity 1 ½ qts.

6135 CASSEROLE
1 ½ qt. Pyrex liner in fluted chrome frame with metal cover.

6141 CASSEROLE
2 qt. capacity Pyrex liner divided into 2 sections. Chrome cover and feet. Diameter 11 in. Overall height 7 in.
6142 CASSEROLE
Same as above but without feet.

6136 PIE PLATE
8 in. Pyrex liner in fluted frame. Diameter 10 in.

Circa 1953

76

Duncan & Miller

Farber Brothers collaboration with Duncan & Miller resulted in a unique line of products which departed from their basic "clip-on clip-off" designs. The Duncan & Miller articles, usually sold in pairs, featured screw-on Farber Bros. bases which doubled as candleholders when the glass was removed. At the present time, five different Farber Brothers items have been identified as having Duncan & Miller inserts, by myself and others. All make use of the screw-on candleholder base, with the exception of two compotes in the Carribean pattern. The compotes, which were sold in a high and low version, were both built from a standard Duncan & Miller 5″ Carribean fruit nappy. A center was drilled in the nappy, and either a stemmed or footed chrome base was then applied.

It appears that inserts crystal in color were primarily purchased. The Carribean compotes have been only found in crystal, although Duncan & Miller produced this line in several colors. The Farber Bros. #200 screw-on base compote pictured can be found in crystal, ultramarine, and crystal with a ruby flashed bowl. By 1953, this compote was only being offered in crystal.

All Farber Brothers items with Duncan & Miller inserts are not easily found, with the exception of the #200 compote with ruby flashing, which has turned up more often than any other piece. The most difficult to find is the 10½″ vase. From the information available, I believe Farber Brothers purchased inserts from Duncan & Miller during the late thirties, forties and even as late as 1955.

200 Compote—Page 128-2, 3
Duncan & Miller. Height 5¾″. Diameter 5½″. Known Colors: Crystal, Ultramarine bowl with crystal stem, Ruby flashed bowl with crystal stem. Screw on base has been only found in chrome. Chrome bases can also be used as separate candleholders. Produced during the 50's, perhaps earlier. *Suggested Value: $15-20.*

6133 Candelabra—Page 129-1
Duncan & Miller. Height 8½″. Width 7″. Known colors: Crystal. Farber Brothers screw on base found in chrome. Chrome base can be removed and used as a separate candleholder. Produced during the early 40's until approximately 1955. *Suggested Value: $60-70/pr.*

"Vases"—Page 129-2, 4
Duncan & Miller. Height 10¼″. Diameter 5¼″. Known colors: Crystal. Farber Brothers screw on base found in chrome. The bases unscrew and can be used as candleholders. *Suggested Value: $70-80/pr.*

"Low Compote"—Page 129-5
Duncan & Miller. Carribean pattern. Height 3½". Diameter 5". Known colors: Crystal. Found in chrome only. Base will occasionally be found unmarked. Produced during the late forties. *Suggested Value: $18-20.*

"Compote"—Page 129-7
Duncan & Miller. Carribean pattern. Height 5¼". Diameter 5". Farber Bros. chrome stem and base with crystal Carribean bowl offered during the late 40's. *Suggested Value: $20-25.*

Fenton

We can give credit to the Fenton Art Glass Company of Williamstown, West Virginia for supplying the bottom half of the butterdish you will find pictured. From the many Farber Brothers items with inserts yet to be identified, Fenton was only able to take credit for this one. Farber Brothers took Fenton's 8″ leaf plate, added a chrome cover and produced a butterdish somewhat out of the ordinary. Traced back to as early as 1940, this butterdish can be found with a ruby or clear satin finish base.

There is some speculation, that the inserts used in the design of items numbered 5782, 5784 and 5785, from the section with glass inserts yet to be identified, were produced by Fenton. Fenton could not confirm or deny this speculation. The leaf design that borders the insert is almost identical to Fenton's Silvertone pressed line. The colors found to date, amber, green, royal blue, ruby and clear satin finish are suggestive of Fenton. I strongly feel that these inserts were produced by Fenton, but hesitate to include them in this chapter until positive proof exists.

5741 Butterdish—Above
Fenton Art Glass Co. Diameter 8½″. Clear satin finish or Ruby 8″ leaf plate topped by Farber Bros. chrome cover with white knob. Offered during the late 30's, into the 40's. A retailer could have bought a dozen of these butterdishes for $9.60 back in 1941. *Suggested Value: Clear satin finish $25-35. Ruby $35-45.*

Fostoria

In the world of collecting, surprises have and always will exist. Just when you think you've seen it all, waiting around the corner is that one piece you never thought existed. This is exactly what happened to me concerning Farber Brothers items with Fostoria inserts. It seemed very likely to me that Farber Brothers purchased inserts from Fostoria during the 30's, 40's and/or 50's, for use in their holders. Fostoria could not find any records to indicate they sold inserts to Farber Brothers. I assumed from what they told me, and due to the fact that no Farber Brothers items with Fostoria had surfaced that this must be true.

But it wasn't true—waiting for me at antique show in Rockland County, New York was the Fostoria American appetizer set you will find pictured. It is the first Farber Bros. item designed using Fostoria inserts that I have encountered in my thirteen year pursuit. I hope it is not the last. Start your collection and you will see that because of the many glass and china companies that supplied inserts, the colors, patterns and etchings used, and the diversity of the items produced, pursuing a collection of Farber Brothers will always be full of surprises.

"Appetizer Set"—Page 129-6
Fostoria Glass Co. American Pattern. Dimensions: Tray 12½″ x 7¾″. Inserts 3″ x 4¼″. Six clear tab handled American inserts set in a chrome Farber Brothers tray with black wooden handles. Fostoria sold a similar item, also called an appetizer set. The inserts sat on a glass tray. *Suggested Value: $45-50.*

Heisey

Using the two Heisey covered dishes pictured on the following pages, Farber Brothers designed several different style butterdishes and even a cheese and cracker dish. These dolphin finial covered dishes can be traced back to 1940 and were supplied to Farber Brothers throughout that decade and for at least three years into the next.

During the early forties, the insert used on item numbers, 5916, 6034, 5892 and 5893 may have been exclusively for Farber Brothers. It is quite possible that this square, dolphin finial, covered dish was not part of Heisey's general line. It neither bears the ⊕ trademark nor appears in Heisey catalogs from that period. This insert is only found in clear.

The insert to the 5743 butterdish, pictured only in clear in Farber Brothers' 1941 and 1953 catalogs, but has been found in Sahara with an almost identical cut design on the cover. I believe this combination to be original. Other colors, such as Flamingo (pink) and Moongleam (green), may have been ordered by Farber Bros.

These are the only Heisey inserts that I have found. Additional colors with items known to exist or new Farber Brothers designs should surface.

5916 Butter or Cheese Dish—Page 129-8
Heisey Glass Company. Dimensions: 9″ x 4½″. Known colors: Crystal. Chrome Duchess Filigree tray. Produced during the early forties. *Suggested Value: $40-45.*

5743 Butterdish—Page 129-10, 11
Heisey Glass Company. Queen Ann pattern. Dimensions: 8½″ x 6″. Inserts in Crystal or Sahara (yellow) with a cut "floral" design on cover, can be found set in chrome trays. Insert bears the Heisey trademark. Heisey marketed this insert as a lemon dish in colors other than Crystal and Sahara. Perhaps other colors than those listed were purchased by Farber Bros. First offered during the 40's until approximately 1953. *Suggested Value: Crystal $50-60. Sahara $65-75.*

5892 Bread and Butterdish—Page 82-Top
Heisey Glass Company. Dimensions: 13¾″ x 7¼″. Known colors: Crystal. This combination bread tray and removable butterdish will be found in chrome. Available during the forties. In 1941, this item was priced at $2.25 each at the wholesale level. *Suggested Value: $40-45.*

5893 Cheese and Cracker Dish—Page 82-Center
Heisey Glass Company. Dimensions: 11¾″ x 11¼″. Known colors: Crystal. Farber Brothers Lafayette design tray made in chrome during the forties. *Suggested Value: $40-45.*

6034 Butterdish—Page 82-Bottom

Heisey Glass Company. Dimensions: 7" x 7". Height 6½". Known colors: Crystal. Farber Brothers butterdish with hexagonal shaped chrome tray and overhanging loop handle was available during the forties. *Suggested Value: $40-45.*

5892

5893

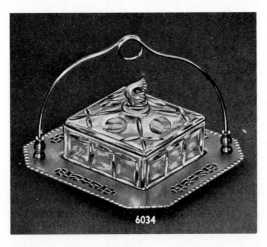

6034

Imperial

Unfortunately, I have not been able to attribute any inserts to The Imperial Glass Company, although research indicates they did supply inserts that were used in Farber Brothers holders. Here is a case where the information needed just isn't available. Records no longer exist from 45 years ago, when Imperial supplied inserts to Farber Brothers. So it is up to us to find out. I am sure as we do more searching, Farber Brothers items with Imperial inserts will surface. Several different inserts from the Candlewick line were supplied to S.W. Farber during the thirties. I suspect this pattern was supplied to Farber Brothers also.

Indiana

In this chapter, are pictured some of the Farber Brothers items designed using glass inserts manufactured by the Indiana Glass Company of Dunkirk, Indiana. Although we don't have an abundance of information on the inserts that were supplied to Farber Bros., we can be sure of one thing—only inserts clear in color were bought from Indiana from the early forties into the early sixties. These clear inserts were placed on several differently styled chrome trays that were ready and waiting to help a busy hostess at her next gathering. These relish dishes and bread trays should not prove difficult to find since many enjoyed a long or late period of production.

A unique Farber Bros. item is the 5846 toast dish. It utilizes a familiar Indiana pattern known to glass collectors as "Daisy". Use it to serve your breakfast toast, pancakes, waffles or, for that matter, anything you'd like to keep warm.

5846 Toast Dish—Above
Indiana Glass Co. #620 line. Commonly called "Daisy" by glass collectors. Diameter of cover 5¾". Farber Brothers chrome cover rests on a clear 9½" plate. Cover is probably unmarked. Produced during the forties, this item sold to retailers for 75 cents in 1941. *Suggested Value: $20-25.*

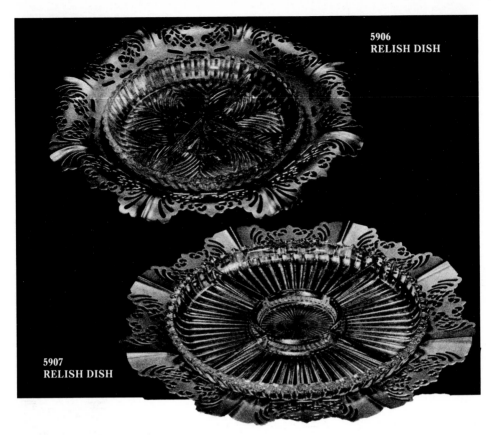

5906
RELISH DISH

5907
RELISH DISH

5906 Relish Dish—Above

Indiana Glass Co. Tray diameter 12″. Diameter of insert 7″. A three compartment clear glass insert sits in a chrome Farber Bros. Duchess Filigree design tray. Produced from approximately 1941 to 1965. *Suggested Value: $18-20.*

5907 Relish Dish—Above

Indiana Glass Co. Diameter 14″. Chrome Duchess Filigree design tray with five compartment removable clear glass insert. Offered during the fifties. A similar item with a four compartment clear glass insert was offered during the forties. *Suggested Value: $18-20.*

5818 RELISH DISH

84

5491 Combination Relish and Bread Tray — Below
Indiana Glass Co. Length 13¼". Width 7". Chrome pierced design tray with three part removable clear glass insert. Produced during the fifties. A similar item was sold during the forties with a handle but minus the glass insert. It used the same item number. *Suggested Value: $18-20.*

5753 Combination Relish and Bread Tray — Below
Indiana Glass Co. Length 13¼". Width 7". Overall height 6¾". Chrome pierced design Farber Bros. handled tray holds a three compartment removable clear glass insert. Produced during the fifties. *Suggested Value: $18-20.*

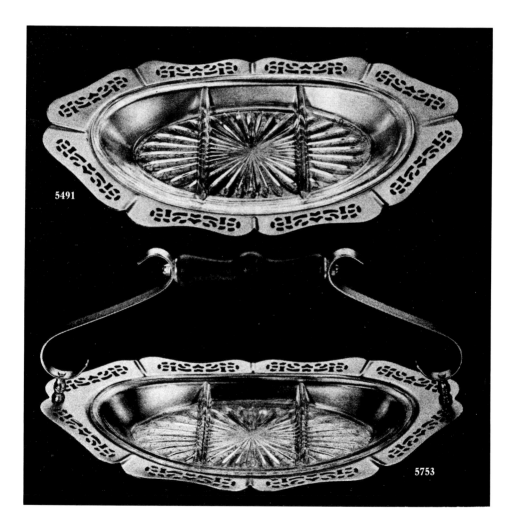

5818 Relish Dish — Left
Indiana Glass Co. #1010 line. Diameter 12½". Farber Brothers chrome tray with five compartments clear glass insert. Produced during the early sixties. *Suggested Value: $18-20.*

New Martinsville

Several years ago, while searching for Farber Brothers items, I came across a New Martinsville Radiance butterbase with a mosaic gold cover. The cover was unmarked, but I was convinced that Farber Brothers purchased the base from New Martinsville, added their own cover and marketed the completed item. A few months later, I found another Radiance butterdish, also unmarked, but this time it had a clear base and a chrome cover of slightly different design. Once again, I felt this was a product of Farber Brothers. For a long period of time, I couldn't find proof that Farber Bros. purchased inserts of any kind from New Martinsville, but then in a Farber Brothers catalog from 1941 I found the proof I needed. Pictured was the clear Radiance butterbase with chrome cover. Finally I could be sure.

You will find butterdishes with clear and light blue Radiance bases with both mosaic gold and chromium plated covers. I have not been able to find these buttercovers with Farber Brothers trademarks. This seems to be the case with most of the covers and lids produced by them. Refer to the chapter on finial shapes to facilitate identification. The butterdishes with mosaic gold covers were produced first, during the mid to late thirties, while butterdishes with chromium plated covers were offered during the early forties. The butterdishes with mosaic gold covers did not enjoy a long span of production. They were dropped before 1941 and therefore are harder to find.

Also produced using New Martinsville glass was a night set in the Janice pattern. It is not easy to find complete and when found whole and in excellent condition will carry a price tag of close to *$60.*

5940 Butterdish—Page 129-9

New Martinsville Glass Company. Radiance pattern. Height 3¼". Diameter 6". Known colors: Clear and Light Blue. Farber Brothers cover found in chrome and mosaic gold. Cover may be unmarked so rely on the shape of the finial for identification. The butterdish with chrome cover is pictured in a 1941 catalog. The butterdishes with mosaic gold covers were the first to be offered. Approximate years of production: Mid to late 30's into the early 40's. *Suggested Value: Chrome $25-35. Mosaic Gold $45-55.*

6064 NIGHT SET — Crystal glass bottle in our patented Clip-On-Off metal holder, crystal drinking glass, scalloped chromium plated tray, dia. 6 in. Height over all 7 in.

6064 Night Set—Above
New Martinsville Glass Company. Janice pattern. Height 7″. Diameter 6″. Known Colors: Clear. Farber Brothers holder and tray found in chrome. Produced during the early forties. Difficult to find. *Suggested Value: $50-60.*

Thermos®

Although not a typical glass insert, as purchased from other glass companies, these genuine Thermos® liners used in Farber Brothers chrome ice tubs are worth mentioning. The reprint shown on the following pages is taken from a 1941 catalog. Compared to many other Farber Brothers items from the same period, these vacuum ice tubs with genuine Thermos® liners could be considered expensive. Wholesale prices ranged from $5.75 for the least expensive D2 vacuum ice tub, to $10.50 for the XD3. These vacuum ice tubs served a dual purpose in many households, by keeping ice cubes from melting for up to 24 hours and by keeping food warm. Several of the chrome ice tubs shown, such as #400, #312C and D6, could be purchased through the early sixties. For those individuals who were tired with the high sheen of chromium, several similar but new designs were offered during the early sixties in solid copper or solid brass, (Page 128-1) with genuine Thermos® vacuum liners. Today, all these ice buckets, whether they are chrome, brass or copper, are offered for sale in the *$25-35*, price range.

IN THE KROME-KRAFT TRADITION OF
ELEGANCE PLUS UTILITY . . . KEEP
CUBES AND COMPANY IN
PERFECT FORM

D2 VACUUM ICE TUB, with genuine thermos liner. Capacity 2 qt. Height over all 8½ in. Walnut side handles and knob.
D3 *(Not illustrated).* Same as above with ice tong attachment and ice tong.

400 VACUUM ICE TUB, with genuine thermos liner. Hammered and plain design, gadroon border. Capacity 2 qt. Height over all 9½ in.

5720 ICE TUB, chromium-plated, with drain and ice tongs. Dia. 6 in. Height over all 8 in. This tub does not have vacuum liner.

XD2 *(below)* VACUUM ICE TUB, with genuine thermos lining. Capacity 2 qt. Gadroon border, combination metal & walnut handles. Height over all 9½ in.
XD3 *(Not illustrated).* Same as above with ice tong attachment and ice tongs.

Page 14

88

Genuine Thermos Liners

Our Vacuum Ice Tubs, which are chromium-plated with genuine Thermos liners, will keep ice cubes from melting for 12 hours and can be used to keep food warm.

399 VACUUM ICE TUB—Capacity 2 qt., genuine thermos lining, wheat border design. Height over all 9½ in.

312C VACUUM ICE TUB—Capacity 2 qt., genuine thermos lining, thread border design. Height over all 9¼ in.

D6 VACUUM ICE TUB—Capacity 2 qt., genuine thermos lining, thread border design. When you press the handle back, the cover automatically lifts up. Height over all 11½ in.

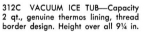

D4 VACUUM ICE TUB—Capacity 2 qt., genuine thermos lining, gadroon border design. Height over all 8½ in.

Page 15

Viking

In 1941, a fire destroyed the records of the Viking Glass Company of New Martinsville, West Virginia. Destroyed were the answers to the many questions regarding which inserts were supplied to Farber Brothers and during which years. The association between the two companies is sketchy, to say the least, but representatives of Viking were able to shed a little light on the subject. They provided me with the following information: During 1941, their #17 oval liner was shipped to Farber Brothers. Despite going to considerable lengths in trying to find a mold, a sample, a picture from an old catalog or a person who could remember the item, Viking could not provide additional information on the #17 oval liner. They were also unable to identify it from among the inserts shown in the chapter covering items with glass inserts yet to be identified. Although we lack detailed records from Viking, we still can positively identify one Farber Brothers/Viking combination. That is the Prelude cake plate shown. As our knowledge grows, we will definitely be able to expand this chapter on Farber Brothers items with Viking inserts.

"Cake Plate"— Page 129-3
Viking Glass Co. Prelude pattern. Height 3½". Diameter 11½". Farber Brothers chrome pedestal base screws on and can easily be removed. Made after 1941. Possibly during the late 40's. *Suggested Value: $50-60.*

Westmoreland

The majority of the Farber Brothers items pictured in this chapter have been designed using a four inch Westmoreland Lotus bowl, as the insert. Compotes, mayonnaises and other accessory pieces all were designed using this one bowl. Most of these items were produced during the 40's and 50's, but a few could still be purchased during the early 60's. By far, the most unique Lotus piece is the centerpiece/lazy susan. It is the only Farber Brothers item I know of that incorporated the products of two different glass companies into one design. Westmoreland supplied the Lotus bowls and Cambridge provided the crystal arms. An extremely interesting member of the Lotus line is the brass/copper compote which is the only known Farber Brothers piece to feature two metal finishes. The compote has a solid brass bowl and a solid copper base and is undoubtedly from the sixties. For versatility, choose the Lotus "candlestick compotes" which are pictured. They can be used as compotes and when you remove the peg nappies, a pair of candlesticks will remain. All Lotus bowls used by Farber Brothers were of two types. Farber Brothers originally used a clear bowl with a frosted finish over the entire glass surface. Approximately 1960, the style of the Lotus bowl changed slightly and the frosted finish was only applied to the exterior of the bowl leaving a smooth finish on the inside.

Farber Brothers also sold a cake basket and a sandwich plate, both of which feature a clear 7 inch Princess Feather plate bordered by a Duchess Filigree frame. Don't pass them by just because they are unmarked. For reasons unknown, these two items will usually be found without a Farber Brothers trademark. A close up of the Duchess Filigree design can be found in the front of the book. Use it as an aid to identify unmarked pieces.

Farber Brothers also purchased a nappy from Westmoreland's #240 line. A clear six inch nappy was drilled in the center and attached to a chrome stem to form a compote.

Farber Brothers items using Westmoreland inserts are plentiful and can be found without much difficulty, with the exception of the "ruffled compote", centerpiece/lazy susan, and the brass/copper compotes. The brass, brass/copper, and silverplated items were produced in limited quantities by Farber Brothers. They are harder to find and should be priced slightly more than their chrome counterparts.

5912 High Compote—Page 130-1

Westmoreland Glass Co. Lotus pattern. Height 7". Diameter 4". Known colors: Clear frosted finish. Holder can be found in chrome, brass and silverplate. Approximate years of production: 1940-1965. This compote is easily found in chrome. Brass and silverplate are harder to find. The silverplate version may have been marketed by Sheffield Silver. Inserts circa 1960 and on, will have the frosted finish on the outside of the insert, with a smooth inside. *Suggested Value: Chrome $15-18. Brass or Silverplate $18-22.*

6115 Centerpiece—Page 130-2

Westmoreland Glass Co. Lotus pattern. Height 8½". Spread 11". Known colors: Clear frosted finish. Farber Brothers candlestick base and peg nappies found in chrome. Produced during the 1940's and early 1950's, this centerpiece has removable nappies which allows the owner to make a variety of arrangements. Peg nappies set in crystal arms supplied by the Cambridge Glass Co. *Suggested Value: $55-60.*

"Compote"—Page 130-3, 4

Westmoreland Glass Co. Lotus pattern. Height 4½". Diameter 4". Known colors: Clear frosted finish. Holder can be found in chrome or the unusual combination of brass and copper. That compote will have a solid brass bowl with a solid copper base. *Suggested Value: Chrome $15-18. Brass with Copper $25-30 each.*

5913 Low Compote—Not Pictured

Westmoreland Glass Co. Lotus pattern. Height 5½". Diameter 4". Known colors: Clear frosted finish. Farber Brothers holder found in chrome. Produced during the 1940's and1950's, this compote sold for $1.35 at the wholesale level in 1941. *Suggested Value: $15-18.*

"Mayonnaise"—Page 130-5

Westmoreland Glass Co. Lotus pattern. Diameter 4". Height 5¼". Known colors: Clear frosted finish. Mosaic gold holder with braided overhanging loop handle. This is probably an early issue from the late 30's. Possibly produced in chrome also. The only piece found to date with a Westmoreland insert in mosaic gold holder, this piece is unmarked. *Suggested Value: $20-25.*

"Candlestick Compote"—Page 130-6

Westmoreland Glass Co. Lotus pattern. Height 5¾". Diameter 4". Known colors: Clear frosted finish. Farber Brothers candlestick base and peg nappy, found in chrome. Produced during the 40's and 50's, these compotes were probably meant to be sold in pairs. The peg nappies are easily lifted off the base to produce a pair of candleholders. *Suggested Value: $30-35/pr.*

5828 ½ Mayonnaise—Page 130-7

Westmoreland Glass Co. Lotus pattern. Diameter 6¼". Height 4½". Known colors: Clear frosted finish. Farber Brothers star shaped tray produced in chrome, brass and silverplate from the 40's until the 60's. Came complete with a mayonnaise spoon. Easily found in chrome. Can sometimes be found without a holder on the Lotus insert. *Suggested Value: Chrome $12-15. Silverplate $15-$18. Brass $18-22.*

5978 Sandwich Plate—Page 131-1
Westmoreland Glass Co. Princess Feather pattern. Diameter 12″. Known colors: Clear. Duchess Filigree design chrome frame will be found unmarked most of the time. Produced during the 40's and possibly into the 50's. *Suggested Value: $18-20.*

5979 Cake Basket—Page 131-2
Westmoreland Glass Co. Princess Feather pattern. Height 6½″. Diameter 12″. Known colors: Clear. Duchess Filigree design chrome frame with overhead handle. Will almost always be found unmarked. Produced during the 40's and 50's. *Suggested Value: $20-25.*

"Ruffled Compote"—Page 131-3
Westmoreland Glass Co. Number 240 pattern. Height 5½″. Diameter 5¾″. Known colors: Clear, Farber Brothers footed stem found in chrome. This compote was designed by taking a nappy, drilling a hole in the center and screwing on a Farber Brothers footed stem. *Suggested Value: $20-25.*

"Chip and Dip Set"—Page 131-4
Westmoreland Glass Co. Lotus pattern. Height 10″. Diameter 13½″. Known colors: Clear frosted finish. Farber Brothers holder found in chrome. Approximate years of production: late 40's and 50's. *Suggested Value: $35-40.*

Farber Brothers Items with Glass Inserts Yet to Be Identified

On the next few pages, are pictured the Farber Bros. items with glass inserts, whose origins, after exhaustive research, have not been identified. The majority of the glass companies that provided inserts to Farber Brothers are no longer in business. Unfortunately, the few that are still in business did not always keep detailed sales records or in some cases, destroyed them long ago. No Farber Brothers records survived after the company dissolved, except for a few catalogs. The catalogs have been extremely helpful in bringing previously unknown items to my attention, but in all instances, no reference is made to the supplier of the insert. With your help, we may be able to identify these inserts and also credit the appropriate manufacturer. Write to me if you recognize any of them.

5785 Compote — Page 132-1, 2, 3
Manufacturer of insert unknown. Possibly Fenton. Diameter 7". Height overall 5¾". Known colors: Clear satin finish, ruby, amber, royal blue and green. Easily found in clear satin finish. Offered by Farber Brothers during the late 30's into the early 40's., in chrome only. *Suggested Value: $25-35.*

"Salt & Pepper Set" — Page 132-4
Manufacturer of insert unknown. Height 4¼". Suggestive of Cambridge Mount Vernon Pattern. Amber or clear inserts set into Farber Brothers chrome holders. Late 40's. *Suggested Value: $18-22.*

6013 Chrome
7013 Brass — Candlesticks — Page 132-5
Manufacturer of insert unknown. Height 5". Known colors: Clear. Farber Bros. holders found in chrome and brass. Produced during the fifties and early sixties. *Suggested Value for chrome or brass: $35-40/pr.*

6993 Chrome
7993 Brass — Candlesticks — Not Pictured. Same insert as 6013
Manufacturer of insert unknown. Height 9". Known colors: Clear. Holders found in chrome and brass. Offered during the late fifties and early sixties. *Suggested Value for chrome or brass: $40-45/pr.*

"Salt & Pepper Set" — Page 132-6
Manufacturer of insert unknown. Height 4¼". Amber or Clear inserts which are similar to Cambridge's Mount Vernon pattern have been found set in Farber Bros. chrome holders. Probably produced during the late forties. *Suggested Value: $18-22.*

5782 Candy Dish—Page 132-7, 8, 9

Manufacturer of insert unknown. Possibly Fenton. Diameter 7". Inserts of clear satin finish, ruby, amber, royal blue and green. Farber Brothers holder and lid found in chrome and mosaic gold. Produced during the late 30's until the early 40's. More difficult to find in mosaic gold. *Suggested Value: Chrome $25-35. Mosaic Gold $40-50.*

"Candleholders"—Page 132-10

Manufacturer of insert unknown. Height 7¾". Diameter 6". These brass candleholders mount on the wall and were originally sold in pairs. They may have been produced in chrome also, with possibly ebony, light blue, blue-green, or even milk inserts found. *Suggested Value: $40-50/pr.*

5784 Basket—Page 133-1, 3

Manufacturer of insert unknown. Possibly Fenton. Diameter 7". Known colors: Clear satin finish, ruby, amber, royal blue and green. Farber Brothers patented holder with overhead handle found in chrome. Produced during the late 30's and the early 40's. Hardest to find in royal blue, green and amber. The other colors are plentiful. *Suggested Value: $30-40.*

6038 Relish Dish—Page 133-2

Manufacturer of insert unknown. Height overall 6¼". Diameter 5¾". Clear insert in Farber Bros. chrome holder. Circa 1940's. *Suggested Value: $10-12.*

"Coasters"—Page 133-4, 5, 6

Manufacturer of insert unknown. Diameter 3½". Known colors: Amber, ebony, light blue and a deep blue-green. Originally sold in sets of 4, one of each color or all one color. Found in chrome holders. Possibly brass holders were made also. These are often advertised as Cambridge, but the blue-green color, suggest they are from another manufacturer. *Suggested Value: Chrome $8-12 each.*

"Preserve Dish"—Page 133-7

Manufacturer of insert unknown. Dimensions: 6¾" x 3¾". Clear and Royal Blue inserts have been found set in a chrome Perforated Lace design tray. Circa 1940's. *Suggested Value: $8-10.*

5914 Relish or Lemon Dish—Page 133-8

Manufacturer of insert unknown. Dimensions: 9" x 4½". Known colors: Clear with frosted bottom. Insert has cut design. Duchess Filigree design holder will be found in chrome. Offered by Farber Bros. during the 40's. Inserts may have been supplied by Corning Glass Works. The cut design is very similar to the designs cut into casseroles supplied by Corning during the same time period. *Suggested Value: $12-15.*

"Preserve Dish"—Page 133-9

Manufacturer of insert unknown. Dimensions: 6¾" x 3¾". Farber Brothers chrome tray with "basket of flowers" design etched on each handle, holds clear glass liner. Produced during the early 40's. A similar item, #6037 preserve dish was also offered in chrome, circa 1941, with an overhead handle and spoon. *Suggested Value for either item: $6-10.*

6039 Pickle Dish—Page 133-10

Manufacturer of insert unknown. Dimensions: 6¾" x 3¾". Height overall 6¼". Known colors: Clear and royal blue. Chrome holder. A similar item was sold without a handle. Both were manufactured during the forties. *Suggested Value: $12-18.*

6032 Buffet Piece—Page 133-11

Manufacturer of insert unknown. Dimensions: 8" x 5½". Height overall 6¼". Known colors: Clear and royal blue. This buffet piece found in chrome, has an overhead loop handle and came complete with fork. Produced during the forties. *Suggested Value: $12-18.*

1

2

3

4

5

6

7

8

9

10

11

12

13

14

Descriptions: Pages 33, 34

1

2

3

4

5

6

7

8

9

1

2 3 4

5

6

Descriptions: Page 39

1

2

3

4

Descriptions: Pages 39-40

1

2

1

2

3

Descriptions: Page 43

1

2

3

Descriptions: Page 43

1

2

Descriptions: Pages 43-44

1

2

Descriptions: Page 44

1   2   3

4   5

6

7   8   9

Descriptions: Pages 45-46

1

2

3

4

5

6

Descriptions: Page 46

1

2

3

4

5

6

7

Descriptions: Page 47

1

2　　　　　　　　3

4　　　　　　　　5

Descriptions: Pages 48-49

1

2

3

4

5

Descriptions: Page 49

Descriptions: Page 50

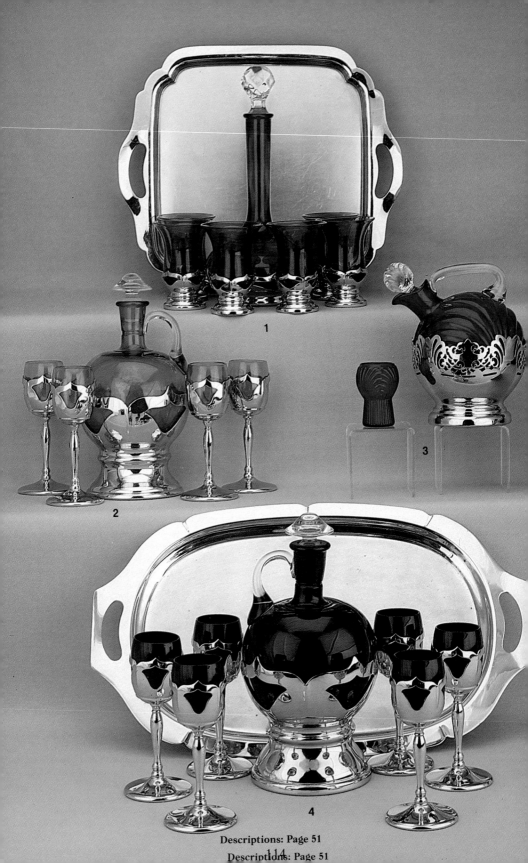

1

2

3

4

Descriptions: Page 51

Descriptions: Page 51

1

2

3

Descriptions: Pages 51-52

1

2

3

Descriptions: Page 52

1

2

3

Descriptions: Pages 52-53

1

2

3

Descriptions: Page 54

1

2

3

4

5

6

7

1

2

Descriptions: Page 58

1

2

Descriptions: Pages 59-60

1

2

3

4

5

6

7

8

9

10

11

1

2   3   4

5   6   7

8   9   10

11

Descriptions: Pages 62-63

1

2

3

4

5

6

7

8

9

10

11

Descriptions: Page 64

1

2

3

4

5

6

7

1

2　　　　　　　　　　　3

Descriptions: Pages 67-77

1

2   3   4

5   6   7

8   9

10   11

Descriptions: Pages 77, 78, 80, 81, 86, 90

1

2

3

4

5

6

7

Descriptions: Pages 91-92

1

2

3

4

Descriptions: Page 96

1   2   3

4   5   6

7   8   9

10

Descriptions: Pages 94-95

1

2

3

4

5

6

7

8

9

10

11

Descriptions: Pages 95-96

1

2

3

Descriptions: Pages 146, 148, 149

1   2   3

4   5

6

7   8   9

Descriptions: Pages 148-150

1

2

Descriptions: Page 152

1

2

3

4

5

6

Descriptions: Pages 154-155

1

2

3

4

5

Descriptions: Page 156

1

2

3

4

5

6

Descriptions: Pages 157

139

1

2

3

4

5

6

7

8

Descriptions: Pages 157-158

1

2

3

4

5

Descriptions: Pages 158-159

1

2

3

4

5

6

Descriptions: Page 159

1

2

3   4   5

6

7

8   9   10

Descriptions: Page 160

1

2   3   4

5

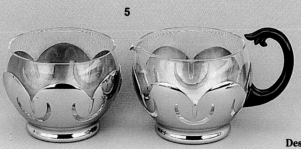

Descriptions: Page 169

Farber Brothers Items with China Inserts

Introduction

The emphasis on Farber Brothers with glass inserts may have caused most collectors and dealers to overlook that they also produced an extensive line of china and pottery accessories to which they added their special accent of metal holders, rims, and bases. Read on and become acquainted with several china manufacturers that supplied the inserts which were used. Fraunfelter China, Lenox China, Harker Pottery, Senegal China and Vernon Kilns are among the list of identified sources for china and pottery inserts. The designs range from the elegance of translucent Lenox accessories to the boldness and practicality of Fraunfelter tea sets. Lenox China was the dominate supplier, producing over 75 percent of all the china inserts used by Farber Brothers. A few items with inserts of unknown manufacture can be found at the end of this section.

Before 1932, Farber Bros. bought relatively small amounts of china to be placed in their holders. Very few items with china inserts can be found pictured in pre-1932 company catalogs, which suggests that little importance was placed on designs that incorporated china or pottery. Before 1932, Farber Brothers primarily manufactured covered casseroles, pie plates, coffee sets, and bouillon sets, in silverplated and nickelplated holders. The majority of all Farber Bros. items with china inserts were produced during the ten year period 1932 to 1942, with the peak of production occurring during the mid to late thirties. The popularity of china had declined considerably by 1941, as a company catalog from that year offers a total of only ten different designs. Interest in these items further declined during the late 40's. Sometime between 1948 and 1950, production of china accessories ceased.

Farber Brothers items with china inserts will be found in holders made out of a variety of metals. They are chrome, silverplate, mosaic gold and nickelplate. All Farber Brothers items with china inserts today prove to be difficult to find, but definitely worth the search.

Fraunfelter China

Fraunfelter China of Zanesville, Ohio provided some of the first china to be put in Farber Brothers patented clip-on clip-off holders. Tea pots, sugars, and creamers in striking, bold colors can be found encased in Farber Bros. chrome holders. The 8 cup tea pot, sugar and creamer, which comprise the tea set pictured, are the only items that have been found using Fraunfelter inserts. Green, orange and black, all with a platinum trim, are the only colors found to date. Farber Brothers purchased Fraunfelter inserts as early as 1932 and possibly as late as 1939. The tea set shown is not easily found and when found, is rarely in mint condition. The platinum trim wore off easily, sugar lids were lost or broken and very often the chrome holders split. Consider yourself fortunate to own one of these sets.

"Tea Set" — Page 134-1

Fraunfelter China. The set consists of a 8 cup tea pot, covered sugar and creamer, set on a 16½" x 9" chrome tray. Sugar cover not shown in photo. Inserts of green, orange or black with platinum trim in Farber Brothers chrome holders were produced from 1932 to possibly as late as 1939. *Suggested Value: $65-75.*

Harker Pottery

Farber Brothers bought china inserts from Harker Pottery of East Liverpool, Ohio as early as 1940. The only inserts that I am familiar with are covered casseroles, in 7″ and 8″ sizes. A 1941 Farber Brothers catalog features these casseroles in pastel pink and pastel blue and refers to them as the Wellesley pattern, although this pattern is known to collectors of Harker Pottery as CameoWare. A catalog reprint of the 7″ size is pictured. In 1941, they were sold to retailers at $2.50 each for the 7″ size and $3.00 for the 8″ size.

6079 7″ Covered Casserole
6080 8″ Covered Casserole—Pictured below
Harker Pottery Co. CameoWare. Farber Brothers chrome holder with a pierced design, contained either a 7″ or 8″ covered casserole. Offered by Farber Bros. during the early forties in pastel pink and pastel blue. *Suggested Value for both sizes and colors: $20-25.*

Lenox China

The only china company still in existence that sold to Farber Brothers is Lenox China. Lenox supplied Farber Bros. with several different china inserts between 1932 and 1940. These inserts were set into holders made of chrome, silverplate and mosaic gold. Mosaic gold are the most readily available.

A green Lenox backstamp ☕ can be found on the underside of each insert. Also located there are item numbers, written in gold ink, which were applied at the Lenox factory. For example—the numbers 2555 and 86B are found on the following items: high compote, covered candy dish, bon bon and double bon bon. The 2555 is the identifying number of the shape of the ware—a fruit saucer. The 86B indicates a $1/16$ inch gold edge was applied to that particular Lenox insert. The other Lenox inserts pictured are also marked with identifying numbers that correspond to the shape of the ware.

Dealers occasionally mistake ivory Lenox china inserts for Cambridge Milk inserts. I have bought several Farber Brothers items with Lenox inserts that were advertised as Cambridge. Lenox inserts are a creamy, ivory color while the Cambridge inserts that Farber Bros. purchased in Milk are a pure snow white. If in doubt, gently snap off the holder and look for the green Lenox backstamp on the underside of the insert.

Most Lenox inserts will be found with either a gold or platinum edge, depending on the color of the holder. Gold edgings with mosaic gold holders and platinum edgings with either the chrome or silverplated holders. The bowl pictured has a platinum edge with a mosaic gold holder. A rather odd combination, perhaps requested by the original purchaser or the result of a replacement insert.

Farber Brothers occasionally put paper labels on the inserts bought from Lenox. A black paper label, with gold lettering, "Farber Bros., N.Y. City. China by Lenox", and a gold scalloped border has been found on several pieces, one of which is the handled salt and pepper.

On the following pages are pictured all the Farber Bros. products with Lenox inserts that I have seen to date. These Farber Brothers/Lenox combinations are not easily found, and when found are priced to reflect their scarcity. Lenox assures me that additional inserts were purchased, so I am certain more pieces will surface in the future.

"Syrup"—Page 134-2; 135-8

Lenox China. 6½" to 6¾" high due to variation in lids. Trimmed ivory inserts in either chrome, silverplate or mosaic gold holders. Note the two different lid styles and china bodies. The silverplated syrup is different from its chrome counterpart in that the lid completely covers the pouring spout and the pouring spout has an "ice lip" effect. *Suggested Value: Chrome/Silverplate $70-80. Mosaic Gold $85-95.*

"Marmalade/Mustard"—Page 134-3

Lenox China. 4¼" to 4½" high depending on finial shape. Ivory insert in Farber Brothers chrome or mosaic gold holders. Possibly silverplate. Note the different finial shapes. *Suggested Value: Chrome $30-35. Mosaic Gold $35-40.*

"Double Bon Bon"—Page 135-1

Lenox China. Height 6½". Diameter 5½". Lenox china ivory insert with gold trim set in mosaic gold holder is the only holder found to date. *Suggested Value: $75-85.*

5562 High Compote—Page 135-2

Lenox China. Height 5½". Diameter 5½". Found in ivory with either a gold or platinum trim in mosaic gold, silverplate or chrome holders. *Suggested Value: Chrome/Silverplate $40-45. Mosaic Gold $45-50.*

"Covered Candy"—Page 135-3

Lenox China. Height 5¼". Diameter 5½". Lenox ivory insert with gold trim set in mosaic gold clip-on clip-off holder. Possibly made in chrome or silverplate also. *Suggested Value: $55-65.*

5560 Bon Bon—Page 135-4

Lenox China. Height 2". Diameter 5½". Ivory insert with gold trim set in mosaic gold holder. Mosaic gold is the only holder found to date. Possibly chrome and silverplate with platinum trim also. *Suggested Value: $40-45.*

"Bowl"—Page 135-5

Lenox China. Height 3½". Diameter 8". Known colors: Ivory with either a gold or platinum trim. Pictured with mosaic gold holder. May have been manufactured in chrome and silverplate also. *Suggested Value: $55-65.*

"Condiment Set"—Page 135-6

Lenox China. Comprised of a sugar, creamer and marmalade on a handled tray. Sugar 3¼" high. Creamer 4¼" high. Marmalade 4½" high. Tray 14½" x 8⅜", may be found unmarked. Ivory inserts with gold trim in mosaic gold holders is the only combination found to date. *Suggested Value: $90-100.*

"Sugar & Creamer"—Pictured as part of Page 135-6

Lenox China. Creamer 4¼" high. Sugar 3¼" high. Ivory colored insert in mosaic gold holders are the only combination found to date. Chrome and silverplate were probably produced also. *Suggested Value: $55-60.*

"Condiment Set"—Page 135-7

Lenox China. Consists of two covered jars set on a 6¾" x 3¾" center handled tray. Can be used for a variety of condiments such as mustard or mayonnaise. Covered jars Height 4½" and 3½". Holders/lids can be found in chrome, mosaic gold and possibly silverplate. *Suggested Value: Chrome $55-60. Mosaic Gold $60-65.*

"Mustard"—Pictured as part of 135-7

Lenox China. Height 3½". Ivory insert in chrome or mosaic gold holders. Discontinued prior to 1940. *Suggested Value: Chrome $25-30. Mosaic Gold $30-35.*

5874 Salt & Pepper—Page 135-9

Lenox China. 3½" high. Ivory Lenox insert with platinum or gold trim. Farber Brothers holder found in mosaic gold and silverplate. Possibly chrome. Salt & Pepper could be purchased with or without tray. Has been found with a paper label that states "Farber Bros.—N.Y. City—China by Lenox". *Suggested Value: Silverplate $35-40 without tray. $40-45 with tray. Mosaic Gold $40-45 without tray. $45-50 with tray.*

Senegal China

Senegal China was a small, Pelham New York based company that was in operation from approximately 1945 until 1951. Farber Brothers reportedly purchased china inserts from them, but no pieces have yet surfaced.

Expect to find small bowls, sugar and creamers, and vases in Farber Bros. holders or set on Farber Bros. bases. Please write me if you can provide additional information on the inserts supplied by Senegal China to Farber Brothers.

Vernon Kilns

Several different size plates from the Moby Dick and Lei Lani series were shipped to Farber Brothers from Vernon Kilns during the late 30's until the early 40's. Using plates in the Moby Dick series designed by Rockwell Kent, Farber Bros. added a chrome frame and produced a versatile item that could be used as either a sandwich plate or plaque. The sandwich plate/ plaque was offered in 12″, 14″ and 16″ sizes. Twelve inch bowls, designed using 6″ Moby Dick plates and a 6″ chrome rim, could also be purchased from Farber Brothers.

The Moby Dick plates supplied to Farber Brothers are different from the Vernon Kilns dinnerware of the same design—they have colored sails, while the dinnerware set does not. This was probably the result of a special request made by Farber Brothers. Although Vernon Kilns marked most of their ware and artist signatures were commonly applied to Kent patterns, the Moby Dick plates supplied to Farber Brothers carried neither a Vernon Kilns mark nor an artists signature. The plates are marked in blue ink on the back, . This mark was applied by Vernon Kilns and is the only mark found on these items. Since the difference in the sail color suggests that these plates were a custom design, it is reasonable to assume that Farber Brothers requested that the Vernon Kilns trademark be excluded.

The sandwich plates/plaques and bowls using plates from the Lei Lani series by Don Blanding are marked differently. Since they were not custom made to Farber Bros. specifications, and were taken from regular stock, they will bear the standard Vernon Kilns Lei Lani trademark with Don Blanding's signature.

The chrome frames that surround each one of the Kent or Blanding plates were offered etched or unetched and often will be lacking a Farber Brothers trademark. Plates from the Salamina pattern, designed by Rockwell Kent, may also be found trimmed in chrome rims, reports Maxine Nelson, author of "Versatile Vernon Kilns" and "Versatile Vernon Kilns Book II".

All Farber Brothers/Vernon Kilns combinations are difficult to find. If you find one, and the price is reasonable, don't pass it by—it may be quite a while before you get a chance to purchase another.

6084 Bowl—Page 136-2, 153
Vernon Kilns. Moby Dick Series. Diameter 12″. Farber Brothers chrome frame found etched or unetched. Offered during the late thirties into the early forties. *Suggested Value: $35-45.*

6088 Bowl—Page 153
Vernon Kilns. Lei Lani pattern. Diameter 12″. Etched or unetched chrome frame. Produced during the late thirties into the early forties. *Suggested Value: $35-45.*

6081 12″ Sandwich or Plaque—Page 153
6082 14″—Page 153
6083 16″—Page 153
Vernon Kilns. Moby Dick series. Made in 12″, 14″ and 16″ diameters. Farber Bros. chrome frame found etched or unetched. Offered during the late 30's into the early 40's. *Suggested Value: $35-55 based on size.*

6085 12″ Sandwich Plate or Plaque—Page 153
6086 14″—Page 153
6087 16″—Page 136-1, 153
Vernon Kilns. Lei Lani pattern. Made in 12″, 14″ and 16″ diameters. Etched or unetched chrome frame. Produced during the late thirties into the early forties. *Suggested Value: $35-55 based on size.*

6084

6087

6086

6085

6081

6082

6083

6088

153

Farber Brothers Items with China Inserts
Yet to Be Identified

In this section are items that have inserts of unknown manufacture. Contact me if you can offer additional information about them.

"Sandwich Plate"—Page 137-1

Supplier of insert unknown. Diameter 11¾". Farber Brothers rim found in chrome. I hope in the near future we will be able to give credit to the supplier of this beautiful plate. It is simply marked on the back "Farber Bros. N.Y.C." in gold lettering. The chrome rim is unmarked. This plate dates back prior to 1932 and was produced during the late 20's into the early 30's. *Suggested Value: $20-25.*

5980 Sandwich Plate—Page 137-2

Supplier of insert unknown. Diameter 12". Farber Bros. Duchess Filigree design rim found in chrome. Available during the early forties. A similar item, #5981 Cake Basket was also produced. It is the same as #5980, but has a chrome handle with ivory colored catalin trim. Listed in a 1941 catalog, the cake basket could be purchased at a wholesale price of $3.50. *Suggested Value for either the cake basket or the sandwich plate: $18-20.*

"Serving Plate"—Page 137-3

Supplier of insert unknown. Diameter 8½". Farber Bros. rim made of chrome. Rim is unmarked. Plate is marked on the back in black ink, Farber Bros. N.Y.C. From all indications, this is an early piece that was probably produced during the late 20's or early 30's. Due to the shape of the blank used, I believe the manufacturer of this plate and the 11¾" sandwich plate to be the same. *Suggested Value: $12-15.*

"Handled Candy Dish"—Page 137-4

Supplier of insert unknown. Diameter 6". Chrome Farber Brothers rim and handle. Rim is unmarked. Underside of the plate is stamped, in gold ink. Produced during the early forties. *Suggested Value: $12-15.*

"Compote"—Page 137-5

Supplier of insert unknown. Diameter 6". Height 4½". Chrome rim, stem and base. Look for the identifying mark on the bottom of the insert and on the underside of the compote base where the stem meets the foot. Produced during the early forties. *Suggested Value: $12-15.*

"Handled Platter"—Page 137-6

Supplier of insert unknown. Dimensions: 14½" x 8¾", inclusive of handles. Platinum edged platter with "floral and bird" design has chrome handles with green mottled catalin trim. An early item, this platter dates back to approximately 1925. *Suggested Value: $20-25.*

5984 Hot Cake or Toast Dish—Below. Same insert as 5980.

Supplier of insert unknown. Diameter 12". Height 3½". Farber Brothers Duchess Filigree design chrome rim with etched chrome cover. Available during the early 40's. *Suggested Value: $20-25.*

5984

Farber Brothers Items Without Glass or China Inserts

Farber Brothers produced many items without using glass or china inserts that deserve your attention. Although primarily found in chrome, many items made from brass, copper, mosaic gold, pewter, silverplate and nickelplate were also produced throughout the fifty years they were in existence. An assortment of these items is presented on the following pages. Pictured are just a few of the many items that are waiting to be found. Versatile, practical and still relatively inexpensive, Farber Brothers items without glass or china inserts will complement your collection.

"Handled Bowl" — Page 138-1
Height 3½". Diameter 9½". Chrome tab handled bowl in the Lafayette design. Difficult to find. *Suggested Value: $18-20.*

5842 Compote — Page 138-2
Height 5½". Diameter 7". Chrome compote with scalloped edge and etched center was produced from the forties through the sixties. *Suggested Value: $6-8.*

5946 Basket — Page 138-3
Height overall 5". Diameter 5". Offered in chrome only during the early forties. Pierced grape design. *Suggested Value: $6-8.*

101 Ashtray — Page 138-4
Dimensions: 3" x 3" x 2½". Solid brass ashtray has intricate ram's head etching in center. Both handled and unhandled versions exist that were originally part of a "stacking ashtray" set. Circa 1915-1920. *Suggested Value: $10-12.*

5954 Nut Bowl Set — Page 138-5
Height 7". Diameter 8". Pierced and etched design. Wood center holds nut cracker and six picks. Produced in chrome from approximately 1940 through 1965. *Suggested Value: $15-18 if complete.*

6119 Candlesticks—Page 139-1, 3

Height 3″. Offered in chrome during the 50's and 60's and perhaps earlier. These candlesticks were the basis for other Farber Brothers compote designs. *Suggested Value: $8-10.*

5465 Serving Tray—Page 139-2

Dimensions: 14″ x 12″. Cutout handles with either an etched or unetched center. Offered in chrome during the late thirties and into the forties. *Suggested Value: $6-8.*

5490 Bread Tray—Page 139-4

Length 13¼″. Width 7″. Farber Bros. pierced design on border with etched center. Produced from the 40's through the 60's in chrome. *Suggested Value: $8-10.*

5982 Bread Tray—Page 139-5

Dimensions: 12″ x 6″. Pierced design with etched center. Offered in chrome from the 40's until the early sixties. *Suggested Value: $8-10.*

5432 Cocktail Set—Page 139-6

Modern hammered and plain design cocktail shaker with black composition handle. 3 pint capacity. Six matching cocktail goblets. 15½″ chromium plated round tray with wheat border design. Offered in chrome during the 40's, 50's and 60's. *Suggested Value: $40-50 set.*

5808 Cocktail Shaker—Page 140-1, 3

Height 12¾″. 1½ qt. capacity cocktail shaker, with orange or walnut colored catalin handle and trimmings. Offered in chrome from the early 40's through the 60's. *Suggested Value: $15-18.*

5300 Cocktail Shaker—Page 140-2

Height 15″. Chromium plated, 2½ quart capacity cocktail shaker with black composition handle was offered by Farber Brothers during the early forties. Your choice of plain or hammered and plain design. *Suggested Value: $20-25.*

5807 Chrome Cocktail Shaker — Page 140-4
7807 Brass
Height 12¾". Capacity 1½ qt. Plain design with metal handle on cover. Produced during the early sixties. Also produced in silverplate by Sheffield Silver during the same time period. *Suggested Value: Chrome/Silverplate $20-25. Brass $25-30.*

5922 10"
5923 12"
5924 14" Vase — Page 140-5
Offered in 10", 12" or 14" heights. Chrome only. Circa 1941. Pictured is the 10" size. One of my favorite pieces. Difficult to find in any size. *Suggested Value: 10" $18-20. 12" $20-25. 14" $25-30.*

5094 Cocktail Shaker — Page 140-6
Height 11". Chrome 1½ quart capacity cocktail shaker with black composition handle. Produced during the early forties. *Suggested Value: $15-18.*

5430 Cocktail Shaker — Page 140-7
Hammered and plain design. Height 11". 1½ qt. capacity with black composition handle. Offered in chrome from approximately 1940 through the sixties. *Suggested Value: $15-18.*

5330 Cocktail Shaker — Page 140-8
Height 11". This 1½ qt. chrome cocktail shaker with black composition handle was offered for over 20 years, from the 40's through the 60's. *Suggested Value: $15-18.*

5666 Handled Plate — Page 141-1, 2
Diameter 12". Farber Brothers chrome handled plate with etched center and Duchess Filigree design border. Chrome overhead handle with black plastic or orange catalin insert. 50's and 60's. *Suggested Value: $12-15.*

5659 ½ Console Bowl — Page 141-3
Height 7". Diameter 11". Etched center with Duchess Filigree design edge. Easy to find. Produced from the 40's through the 60's in chrome only. Called #5659 during the 50's and 60's. *Suggested Value: $15-18.*

5810 Plate — Page 141-4
This Duchess Filigree design 12" plate was offered by Farber Bros. in chrome only during the 50's. Same as #5666, only minus the handle. *Suggested Value: $6-8.*

5660 Centerpiece and screen — Page 141-5

Diameter 11½". Height 5". Produced in chrome during the 40's. Duchess Filigree design border. *Suggested Value: $25-35.*

5961 6"
5962 7½" Compote ("Nude Stem") — Page 142-1, 6

Pierced grape design. Two sizes, 6" and 7½" high. Chrome. Offered during the early 40's. A similar item in 6" and 7½" sizes, with the same catalog number was offered during the 50's and 60's. A plain stem replaced the "nude stem". *Suggested Value: "Nude Stem" 6" $15-18.*
                          7½" $18-20.
          Plain Stem   6" $8-10.
                         7½" $10-12.

5650 12"
5651 14"
5652 16" Service Plates — Page 142-2

Duchess Filigree design edge with etched center. 12", 14", and 16" sizes were offered by Farber Bros. from the 40's through the 60's. *Suggested Value: 12" $6-8. 14" $8-10. 16" $10-12.*

"Double Compote" — Page 142-3

Height 6¾". Diameter 12½". This "double compote" in Perforated Lace design has a wooden black lacquered base. Not an easily found item. *Suggested Value: $20-22.*

5667 Cake or Sandwich Tray — Page 142-4

Diameter 14". Height 6½". Duchess Filigree design tray with etched center, has walnut or orange colored catalin center handle. Offered during the late thirties into the early forties. *Suggested Value: $18-20.*

5508 Chrome Compote — Page 142-5
7508 Brass

Diameter 6". Height 4½". Perforated Lace Design. Produced in chrome from the 40's into the 60's. Brass version was offered only during the late 50's and early sixties. *Suggested Value: Chrome $6-8. Brass $10-12.*

"Cake or Sandwich Tray"—Page 143-1

Dimensions: 11¾" x 11" x 6". Chrome tray with center handle of orange colored catalin. Produced during the late 40's. *Suggested Value: $12-15.*

5705 Water Pitcher—Page 143-2

Height 7". Diameter 5½". 2 qt. capacity. Chromium plated with ice guard. Walnut or orange colored catalin trimmed handle. Also sold without an ice guard, item #5705 ½. Circa 1941. *Suggested Value $15-18.*

"Tumbler"—Page 143-3, 5

Height 2". Capacity 2½ oz. This "double banded" tumbler was offered during the late forties and was sold in set of six or eight. *Suggested Value: $5-6 each.*

"Water Pitcher"—Page 143-4

Height 8¼" to top of handle. 2 qt. capacity. Offered by Farber Brothers during the forties and perhaps later in chrome. Black composition handle. *Suggested Value: $15-20.*

5202 Double Vegetable Dish—Page 143-6

Length 12". Width 9". Produced in chrome from approximately 1930 until the early sixties. Farber Brothers Lafayette design. *Suggested Value: $12-15.*

5058 Chrome Sugar and Creamer Tray—Page 143-7
7058 Brass

Dimensions: 10" x 15". Chrome or brass with etched center offered during the mid 50's until the 60's. *Suggested Value: Chrome $4-6. Brass $6-8.*

5668 Candlesticks—Page 143-8

Height 8". Base 3½". These chrome "Nude Stem" candlesticks were offered during the 40's with a glass candle cup. The all chrome version pictured could be purchased during the fifties. *Suggested Value: All chrome $30-40/pr. With glass insert $60-65/pr.*

5505 Chrome Tidbit—Page 143-9
7505 Brass

Height 8". Diameter of each tray 6". Perforated Lace Design. Chrome produced during the 40's through the 60's. Brass produced late 50's, early 60's. *Suggested Value: Chrome $8-10. Brass $10-12.*

5840 Bon Bon—Page 143-10

Diameter 7". Etched design. Center handle topped with white knob. Offered in chrome during the forties. *Suggested Value: $6-8.*

Farber Brothers Advertisements

The majority of Farber Brothers advertisements can be found in prominent women's magazines from the late forties and early fifties. The following ads were taken from Better Homes and Gardens and American Home. Additional advertisements can be found with a little searching in House and Garden and Woman's Home Companion from the same time period. The advertising firm of Mumm, Mullay and Nichols of Columbus, Ohio was responsible for developing Farber Brothers' ad campaign during the forties.

... LOVELY
ACCESSORIES
IN SMART,
MODERN
FORM

Lustrous chrome that
never tarnishes and sparkling
inserts of fine, hand-made
glass in distinctive colors,
combined in modern design for
gracious entertaining . . . and
for perfect gifts. Mountings snap off
for easy cleaning or replacement
of the glass . . . At better
gift departments everywhere.

SNAPS OFF

SNAPS ON
(pat'd)

created by Farber Bros., New York, N. Y.

American Home
November 1946

gifts with a brilliant future

Smart, Krome-Kraft accessories
like this sugar-creamer . . . in
lustrous chrome that never tarnishes, combined with sparkling
inserts of fine hand-made glass
in distinctive colors. Patented
mountings protect the glass,
snap off for easy cleaning or
replacement. At better gift and
department stores.

SNAPS OFF

SNAPS ON
(pat'd)

FARBER BROTHERS, New York, N. Y.

American Home
January 1947

Krome-Kraft
FARBER BROTHERS

to truly reflect your hospitality

Sparkling hand-made glass in distinctive colors, and finest non-tarnishing chrome in all its lustrous beauty. Patented chrome mountings snap off for easy cleaning and replacement. At gift, jewelry and dep't stores.

Snaps off   **Snaps on**
                        (pat'd)

FARBER BROTHERS
17 Crosby St., New York, N. Y.

Smart sets
for modern tables

Salt-and-peppers of striking beauty. Tilted style 2½ in. high. Uprights 3½ in. high. Glass in amber or amethyst.

Distinctive Krome-Kraft accessories, prized for decorative as well as practical uses. Quality chrome holders protect the sparkling inserts of fine handmade colored glass — snap on and off for easy cleaning. At better gift, jewelry and department stores.

Snaps On

Snaps Off
(Pat'd Feature)

Krome Kraft
FARBER BROTHERS

17 Crosby St., New York, N. Y.
"DISTINGUISHED FOR QUALITY"

Table Gems

of chrome and fine glass. For bright tables and thoughtful giving — this lovely condiment set of non-tarnishing chrome and fine, hand-made glass, merged in beauty on a handsome tray. Write for folder. See Krome-Kraft's table and beverage services at gift, jewelry and dep't. stores. Farber Bros., 17 Crosby St., New York.

Krome·Kraft
£ 🦞 ⚜
FARBER BROTHERS

Snaps on   Snaps off

Patented holder protects glass — makes cleaning easy.

Cruets 3¾ in. Salt and peppers 2½ in. high. Color: amber or amethyst.

"DISTINGUISHED FOR QUALITY"

Better Homes & Gardens
December 1947

Right for Bright tables

A KROME-KRAFT CONDIMENT SET

Sparkling holders of quality chrome, with gay jugs of fine colored glass. To spice up your table—and as a most practical gift. At Jewelry, Gift and Department Stores. Write for folder. Farber Brothers, 15 Crosby St., New York, N.Y.

Krome·Kraft
£ 🦞 ⚜
FARBER BROTHERS

Snaps off   Snaps on

(pat'd)

Patented holder protects glass — makes cleaning easy.

Cruets 3¾ in. Salt and peppers 2½ in. high. Color: Amber or Amethyst.

"DISTINGUISHED FOR QUALITY"

Better Homes & Gardens
May 1948

164

brilliance and Color
for every-day service

Typical of Krome-Kraft's many unique, practical table accessories are these sparkling creamer & sugar and salt & pepper sets in lustrous non-tarnishing chrome combined with fine hand-made colored glass. Mountings protect glass, snap off-on for cleaning. Grand gifts! Gift, jewelry, department stores. Send for folder.

Snaps off

Snaps on

(patented feature)

FARBER BROTHERS
15 Crosby Street, New York City
"Distinguished for Quality"

Better Homes & Gardens
November 1948

Tasteful
for smart tables

Enjoy the modern beauty of lustrous chrome and fine hand-made glass combined in practical Krome-Kraft table accessories of distinctive design! Shown are relish dish, and oil and vinegar set . . . so perfect for your table, and for gifts! At gift, jewelry and department stores. Send for free folder.

snaps on
snaps off
(pat.)

Krome-Kraft
FARBER BROTHERS

FARBER BROTHERS
15 Crosby St., New York City
"Distinguished for Quality"

Bright Ideas

to make your table smart and colorful

But two of many distinctive Krome-Kraft innovations in lustrous, non-tarnishing chrome and fine hand-made colored glass! Patented chrome mountings protect glass, snap on-off for easy cleaning. Superb gifts! At jewelry, gift and department stores.

snaps off   snaps on

(patented feature)

Krome Kraft
£ 🏵 ⚜
FARBER BROTHERS

FARBER BROTHERS
15 Crosby St., New York
"Distinguished for Quality"

Better Homes & Gardens
September 1950

American Home
December 1950

Gift-glamour

in chrome-and-fine glass

Discriminating hostesses hail this versatile Krome-Kraft Lazy Susan, with clear crystal or colored glass set in protective chrome holders . . . holders that snap off and on for easy cleaning! The delightful relish dish also combines non-tarnishing chrome with sparkling glass. Choose them and other Krome-Kraft creations for perfect gifts. At leading jewelry, gift, department stores.

Krome-Kraft
£ 🏵 ⚜
FARBER BROTHERS

Snaps Off   Snaps On

(patented feature)

FARBER BROTHERS
15 Crosby St., New York
"distinguished for quality"

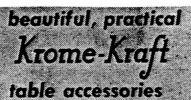

beautiful, practical
Krome-Kraft
table accessories

jam jar

creamer & sugar set

Snaps On   Snaps Off
(patented feature)

You'll love these unique, ever-so-smart Krome-Kraft table accessories with their fine hand-made colored glass inserts and detachable non-tarnishing chrome mountings! Easy to clean—always bright and attractive! For you to see at good stores everywhere.

FARBER BROTHERS
15 Crosby St., New York City
"Distinguished For Quality"

Better Homes & Gardens
February 1951

Farber Brothers Look-Alikes

Beware! They are out there and look close enough like Farber Brothers items to fool the beginning collector.

Take a look at the two Farber Brothers "look-alike" salt and pepper sets with glass inserts. Made in Japan and marked as such on the bottom of each holder, these salt and pepper shakers as well as cruets and condiment sets can be found in a variety of colors. Light green, amber, cobalt and amethyst being the most common, in holders of chrome, aluminum and nickelplate. Farber Brothers was aware of their existence but no action was taken to stop the production of these items. Page 144-2, 3.

Pictured is an unmarked cocktail set, which consists of a chrome cocktail shaker and six cocktails, set on a rectangular tray. The glass inserts to these cocktails can be found in amethyst, amber, emerald green and smoke grey, sometimes bearing a Morgantown Glassworks label. The manufacturer of the chrome holders, tray and cocktail shaker is still uncertain at this time, since they do not bear identifying marks, but may have been produced by United Chromium of Brooklyn, New York. Several companies were said to have copied the clip-on clip-off holder design after the patent rights had expired. Page 144-1.

Glass coffee makers, sugars and creamers having chrome holders and clear glass inserts, were marketed by The Silex Company during 1940. Each sugar and creamer is marked on the bottom, "LICENSED UNDER PAT. No. 1924011" and can be found with either black or ivory plastic handles and trim. There are many similarities between these chrome holders and those produced by Farber Brothers. It is quite possible that Farber Bros. furnished holders to Silex during the early 40's, or they may have been manufactured by another company that paid for the right to use the patented clip-on clip-off holder design. Page 144-5.

Also pictured is a set of salt and pepper shakers that will probably never confuse you into thinking they were made by Farber Bros. These all metal shakers are just another example of the many companies that tried to use the popularity of the clip-on clip-off design to their advantage. Page 144-4.

INDEX

171

INDEX
By Farber Brothers Catalog Numbers

REFERENCES

I recommend highly the following books and publications which aided my research on Farber Brothers.

National Cambridge Collectors, Inc., Colors in Cambridge Glass, 1984.

Hazel Marie Weatherman,
  Colored Glassware of the Depression Era 2, 1974.

Mary, Lyle and Lynn Welker, The Cambridge Glass Co.
  Reprints of Old Company Catalogs Books I and II, 1970, 1974.

Bill and Phyllis Smith, Cambridge Glass 1927-1929, 1986.

National Cambridge Collectors, Inc.,
  The Cambridge Glass Co. 1930-1934, 1976.

William Heacock, Fenton Glass, The Second Twenty-Five Years, 1980.

Maxine Nelson, Versatile Vernon Kilns, 1978.

Last but not least . . .

Perhaps you have found a Farber Brothers item that is not listed, one that is, but in an unlisted color, another old advertisement, or maybe you just want to talk about your collection. You can contact me at P.O. Box 5301 North Branch, N.J. 08876. Please enclose a self addressed stamped envelope if you want a reply. I'll be waiting to hear from you.